ANTHOLOGIA

A COLLECTION OF STORIES BY WOMEN

DANIELLA LIBRI ELIAS, ROSE MASCARO, BENITA BENSCH,
COURTNEY ZERAFA, KELLIE HANNAH, S. JO-ANNE,
JOANNE WILLMOTT, JACQUELINE GAUL, ZOE PERRY,
ELIZABETH HAMMANG, KRISTINA GARLA, S. A. SISIKA,
JACQUI DOYLE, DONNA WALSH, STACEY HOWES, CLAUDIA CALLISTO,
NATARSHA WILSON, CHRISTIE-LEE DIDOVICH, EMMA RIGNEY,
NATALIE SIMES, ASHLEE CANDY SAM, SARAH ROSS

ISSUE 2

ANTHOLOGIA

A COLLECTION OF STORIES BY WOMEN

THE
KIND
PRESS

First Published in 2025 by The Kind Press

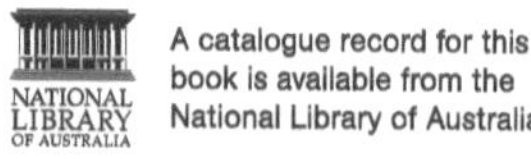

Paperback ISBN 978-1-7638009-7-7

The Kind Press acknowledges all Aboriginal and Torres Strait Islander Traditional Custodians of Country and recognises their continuing connection to land, sea, culture and community. We pay our respects to Elders past and present.

www.thekindpress.com

To all women everywhere

INTRODUCTION

The word anthology comes from the Greek word anthologia, meaning flower gathering, from 'anthos' (flower) and 'legein' (to gather, to select), and entered English in the early 17th century, keeping its metaphorical sense of a carefully selected assemblage.

Anthologia stands in that tradition, a gathering of women's voices, each singular yet placed side by side, enduring together.

Women have always written. Even when our words were pushed to the margins, hidden in letters, confined to diaries, whispered between generations, they endured. To write has always been to resist erasure. Our words carry memory, and with memory, defiance. They carry revolt, and with revolt, vision. They carry the wisdom of those who came before us. The first story ever told was a woman's voice, carrying the knowledge of survival, the ache of loss, and the wonder of life itself. They were the witches, the storytellers, the keepers of memory and imagination. The women in these pages, like the women before them, have always known how to endure and carry vision.

This issue features twenty-two vital contributions in fiction, non-fiction, and poetry, written with verve and clear insight. The work is grounded in personal experience, and often the writers explore the broadest possible meaning, so that the experiences become universal. These pieces are at once powerful, tender, and intimate, allowing the reader rare access to the very core of transition. Together, they form an engaging and emotionally resonant collection.

To write is never only to record. It is to cast light. It is to take the world as it is and see it anew. It is to honour the selves we have been, and to allow space for who we are still becoming. From long lines of women's knowledge, we grew. And still, we grow.

Each page underscores the urgency of documenting our lives for a braver, kinder, more beautiful world. In uncertainty, when change is relentless, stories guide us to strong ground. They remind us what it means to be human, and why our voices matter.

May you lose yourself and find yourself somewhere, if not everywhere.

A VESSEL OF CREATION

DANIELLA LIBRI ELIAS

For the mothers of creativity,
may your love always reach the hearts that need it most.

There was a static in the air, a charge. A low crackle sent a wave of energy through our silent pause. I knew this was one of those significant moments. A signpost placed on my soul's path – imprinted and final. We sat on opposite sides of the lounge, with little left to say. Our eyes met, both brimming with sad acceptance. We exhaled together, deep and long. For fourteen years, we embraced each day with a hope that never imagined this, and now, for the first time, we confronted our reality aloud.

'So … that's it? Are we closing this chapter?' My voice surprised me. It was strong, without a waver. It betrayed none of the emotion I held.

'Yeah … it is what it is.' He looked and sounded exhausted, nine months of self-questioning heavy on his shoulders.

From the moment we became *we*, a family was always part of the vision. We spoke our intentions on that very first date. All on the table. It was clear, never questioned. Not once. That's the thing about being human, right? We plan and plan, believing we have control, but we never really do. The many tests did bring us to our answer, though. It filled us with grief and relief at the exact same time. So that's the reason. It isn't our fault, just the genetic lottery dealing its hand, revealing the play in an unexpected way. Completely out of our control.

'No kids then,' I said, just one more time, to confirm.

'No,' his soft-spoken voice filled with reverence. He looked up and held my gaze. 'Do you still love me?'

A heartfelt huff escaped my lips as I crawled into his arms, my safe cocoon. We were tied, he and I. Timeless to say lifetimes, but when it is your truth, it is your truth. There was not an inch of me that did not feel firmly bound to this man. He waited, patiently, the slightest hint of fear in his eyes, almost holding his breath. As if the words I would say could express anything other than the deep adoration I felt.

'My heart beats for you. Can't you hear it? The heart does not lie. I will always love you.'

~

Time wrapped around me in ribbons. Thousands of layers spiralling in motion, each flowing through a journey, their narratives unfolding. The ribbons that glowed gold were only visible to those who knew where to look. They quivered with a gentle vibration. One that allowed them to exist on their own plane, while also pulsating alongside one another. Past, present, and future all at once. I sat in the middle with my legs crossed, my favourite jeans and crisp white tee a stark contrast to the layers of memory dancing in front of my eyes. Each held a rawness, scattered and unpredictable. In this moment, I was the most put-together I had been in a very long time. My hair was so long it draped across my shoulders in the darkest of waves. My skin was sun-kissed from the hours spent pondering life outside. There was a new lightness that skimmed my aura; it felt cool to touch, fresh. My mind was not choked with thought, but finally clear with a spaciousness I welcomed.

As my eyes glazed across the floating memories, I noticed threads of ribbon that had a deeper glow. Not exactly dull in colour, just different. If you squinted hard enough, you could narrow the gaze to the days that were clouded by my grief. A mourning for the emptiness of my womb. Death of the future I envisioned, one that no longer belonged to me. You could see my hand trying its hardest to keep up with the rapid flow of inner dialogue pouring out through the ink. Stains and smears across illegible words. *How was it that the inner mother told me that I was ready to hold, carry and birth? She told me to prepare, and yet, here we are now, it is not even part of my path. Why? I don't understand.*

Another ribbon, another layer of time dancing above. The tears. Oh, the tears. The buckets they could fill. Uncontrollably, they would escape me in warm bursts. Not just fuelled by sadness, it was more. Deeper. Something I didn't want to admit and took what felt like forever to understand. But it was unmistakable. It was relief, yes, a full-body exhale. Relief that I got a pass. That none of those big decisions would ever be mine. That I would now discover what I wanted without restriction. Bittersweet, the relief that stirred the most shame.

If you looked slightly to the left, tilting your head a little, your eyes would notice a ribbon slicked with tears, another of uncontrollable weeping. Messy thoughts in their most exposed state. That night, I opened up to my friends after months of holding it all in. It was not classified, so to speak, simply an untold truth that my love and I were not ready to share, not while we were still integrating. That evening, though, as I cried, I did not shy away. I did not apologise. Not even one tissue was used. I let every tear take up the space it needed. Allowing the full force of my expression to be seen and received. To be truly held by women who were there to witness me without judgment. What a gift. It was there that I came to terms with not having to do it alone.

I took a deep inhale, bringing my mind back to the present, slowly rotating my hands around the tiny, well-worn sneakers. For years, the sneakers were kept in a box in my parents' roof. Eventually making their way to me. They were once mine after all. And now, two pairs for the two girls I envisioned. No, not just envisioned, but connected with. I wrapped them carefully with tissue paper. Gently placing them back in the storage box. *Should they be donated? Is it weird that I am holding on to them?* Upon receiving them, my sentimental self had put them aside, taking their resurfacing as a sign. In reality, though, things only ever have the meaning that we choose to give them, so the shoes were not a sign; they were simply a reflection of the hope I held.

I pushed the box to the back of the cupboard, wondering how long it would be before I stumbled upon them again. But that's it. The last of it. The shoes were the final piece to check off a very long list. A list that started with a purposeful scroll through my phone. Mass deletion of saved folders. One for pre-conception. One for pregnancy. Another for post-partum and beyond. Being prepared has always been my default, so one can only imagine the depth of these digital homes for all my curiosities. I cleared the list of local midwives, the birth plan and screenshots. Threw out the tinctures from my naturopath, cancelled the acupuncture and the womb massage.

All tabs officially closed.

It still amazes me the way we absorb expectations so easily and make them our own. Wearing them as beliefs, as dreams. Forgetting to use our hearts to guide us through the moulds we have been placed in. Not trusting our intuition to determine whether the checkboxes we are told to tick are even aligned with our desires.

Everything is expected to fit neatly. To make sense. To fall into place. Amongst all the rhetoric, we accept the stories as gospel for all. No wriggle room left for an alternate way of being or thinking. No care for the deepest longings that live beneath the acceptable paths. I found myself childless, yet with all the maternal energy flowing through my veins – a perplexed inner battle within as I had moved through the motions of my days.

A particular ribbon caught my eye. Distracting me, yet again. I could see myself, a little fuzzy, but unmistakably me, pacing amongst the threads. I was angry there. My body burned as if fire were being released through every pore. I could feel the betrayal dripping, betrayal by my inner mother for her lack of warning. We all have the Mother archetype within. She is the energetic signature of the second phase of a woman's life cycle, reigning from twenty-five to fifty. I thought I knew her. I spent so much time building a deep connection to her. Visiting through meditation. Channelling through my journal. Constant communication back and forth. She, like the other archetypes, guides me through the endless spirals of life. Helping to connect deeper with myself, to understand experiences and honour what I need. Usually, I get to feel a sacred presence and collective wisdom when I tune in to her whispers.

The inner mother's energy is deeply nurturing and warm. She grounds herself in an ever-flowing, unconditional kind of love. So abundant in birthing creations as this creativity is part of her natural state. She moves with a rare form of practicality, understanding, and compassion. And when we reclaim her, along with all that she stands for, we reclaim ourselves. The inner mother holds so much that she, too, needs to be held. But I did not want to hold her. She had breached my trust. I had all this energy and did not know where or how to channel it, and she was who I blamed because it was *her* that I was mirroring. Of course I was. She was who I identified with most. Her energy poured through so much of what I do. The inner mother does not in any way try to replace the sheer potency of the physical mother bond. No, that can never be replicated or overtaken. That exists in its own realm. But the *energy* of the inner mother resides within all, whether we know it or not. My inner mother was begging to be expressed.

The more I followed the length of ribbon, the more I withdrew. I witnessed closing my crown, turning the volume down on her, cutting off access. At first, it was to ignore the parts of self that wanted to come out, but eventually it became something else. A much-needed descent into the void. Retracting completely until there were no more shadows to wade through. The void is not seen; it is a feeling. It is all-encompassing and goes on for so long that the ribbon holding it seems to move in an uninterrupted, never-ending path. The length we stay varies. It was in the between, surrounded by quietness, that I had no choice but to confront the truths that are only ever found in solitude. There, I witnessed the layers of my reflection, new depths being expressed. I was able to look not with judgment, but quiet observation, and eventually, even the hardest of hurts became seeds that I knew would grow into something brilliant. The greatest realisation in the void was that none of this had to be a restriction. Not bearing children isn't a limitation on my journey, it's simply a part of it.

The ribbons don't make a sound. Even so, there was one above that rustled, directing me away from the memories of the void and transporting me to a workshop held in the most beautiful of tents. Every inch was draped in lush reds and pinks. There were velvet lounges and plush rugs. The Womb Temple, they called it. We had gathered to hear the wisdom of Jane Hardwicke Collings, who was sharing on the Spiritual Practice of Motherhood. Why I felt called to attend, knowing that I would not be a physical mother, was not something I questioned. I just knew I needed to be there. I had been in a state of integration for so long, finally coming to terms with knowing my inner mother once more – my olive branch to her.

I could see women of all ages and stages of life, gentle smiles were passed, and before we knew it, we were listening to Jane, sharing and holding red twine in our hands. With the twine, we began to tie knots – a symbolic nod to our lineage. The number of knots you had depended on how many pregnancies you had had in your life. It began with the first knot for menarche, our first bleed. Knots for conceptions and births. For those who had completed their family, they closed the thread with a final tie, as did the women who were choosing to stay childless. Two knots for me. One for menarche and one closing the cycle. It was beautiful. An acknowledgement I didn't know I needed. With the many variations that surrounded me, each woman proudly holding their red threads, I reflected on how powerful it was to be on our own path, all with our lessons, perspectives, and impact. How incredible that we can come together along the way and connect over such varied, yet shared experiences. The magic of womanhood.

As we tied our knots, Jane's words filtered through my mind. 'For the aunties here, *be* the Aunty as we recreate the village. We need the village.' I thought of my twenty nieces and nephews. My sisters, my sisters-in-law, and the selfless love of the mothers among us. The millions of ways they are stretched as they raise the children. It truly is incredible. The love of a mother is unlike anything that exists, an energetic chord, undeniable. I still need and want my mother. I see it in the way my mother mourns the loss of her mother; a bond so deeply rooted, I don't believe it can ever be truly broken. Jane's words sat with me as the workshop went on. The village is not only craved but deeply needed. We need to get comfortable expanding the use of our inner mother's energy to be of service to the physical mothers as well. To hold them the way they hold others. More and more, I could see the crucial role I was here to experience. The connections I hold to my nieces and nephews are very different from those of their mothers, but they, too, are essential, valued. The more I resonated with the words, understood there is a need for all, the more my heart began to mend, my perspective slowly shifting.

'And make no mistake, to be in your summer, in your creative, you are also in the energy of the mother. Your space is still important in the collective process,' she said.

And that was it.

The sharp inhale I took brought tears to my eyes.

In the void, I closed off the connection to my inner mother even though I felt she was begging to come through. I silenced her without giving her any opportunity to say *how* she wanted to be of service, what *she* needed to feel expressed. What Jane said was rekindling the fire I had squashed within. *Dig deeper*, it said. *Come back to your roots. Your heart. Your creativity.*

Before I left that day, I spoke to Jane, mentioning my many nieces and nephews, and she looked me in the eyes, and with a strong voice, said, 'You've got important work ahead.' That was the verbal hug my soul was waiting for. Understanding completely taking root.

Worthy.

Enough.

Needed.

Those words helped me towards a light that made me feel like I was re-emerging newly born, ready for what lay ahead. It was clarity that met me at the surface. Patiently waiting as if it had been there all along. Of course, once I emerged, the mother archetype became louder and louder. She pounded on her drum. Made as much noise as she could and chanted until I listened. Truly listened. She forced me to see the very real existence of her within me. In closing off from her and muffling her connection, it only made me shrink myself into a version that felt placeless. I did that to myself because I believed the story that there is more value to a physical mother than a woman who is not. Forgetting that internally, we all have access to the energy of the archetype that allows us to tap into that deep well of all the mother encompasses. It was time to show devotion to the inner mother, because not expressing her was rejecting a part of myself.

Suddenly, all I could feel was a deep need to do something, to bring something, to birth something into this world. It was shaking me from within. That was her coming through, my inner mother, even when I had closed myself off to her, beneath the surface, she was still nurturing my dreams. She was picking inspiration from the portal of creativity and sprinkling it around me. She was planting seeds and romanticising my hopes to fill me with possibility. The more I allowed myself to crack open to her again, the more I could see.

One last ribbon, the final I would tune into for the day. I could see myself curled up in bed, deep in slumber. At that point, the tug from the inner mother had felt the strongest it ever had. It was all I could think about. *Keep going,* she said. *The womb is the holder of all your ideas, all your creations.* I could feel the need to take action. It was time I shifted my own inner narrative to allow the creative within me to be re-imagined. I dreamt of Celestina that night. A character of mine who holds a special place in my heart. She had come to me months earlier. A whole story birthed through another dream. Her inspiration channelled through my core, and from the moment I woke, she was penned onto a page. She was my age, the mirror to the inner mother, and I instantly connected to her. I knew she was destined for a story still untold. She felt like mine.

On this night, though, when she returned, she was different. It was like my subconscious was communing with my creative muse, letting it speak, showing up for the part of me that I had left alone for far too long. There she was. Celestina, but in her maiden form, much younger than she had been the first time. Not that it stopped me recognising her, she was a part of me in a way I could not explain. She looked serene, so sweet. Her curly hair was all over the place, small bouncy ringlets flying in the wind. Almond-shaped eyes and freckles splattered like stars across her nose. She was younger. When I asked her why, she said most matter-of-factly, 'Because I wanted to remind you that you are my mother. I need your love, your nurturing. The older Celestina wouldn't come and tell you this, so I am here.'

It hit me then, the importance of the creations I hold inside. She wanted me to continue writing. She wanted me to bring her into this world. To allow her to exist outside of my brain. My heart felt full waking up and I knew exactly what to do. There was no more sadness lingering. No quiet retraction needed. I did not go to the emptiness of my womb because finally, my womb felt full.

Day by day, I returned to myself. The more I showed up for my inner mother through my creative outpour, the more I felt like me. The vision was clear. There will be daughters born of my devotion. They might not be destined to come earthside in physical form, but birthed through my inner world – their energetic imprint will be deeply marked on the creations that come forth. I will make sure of it. I will write their names. I will let their features mirror my own. I will cloak them with the wisdom I have and allow them to be the voices that carry it on. They will hold my red thread regardless, and I will witness their growth and their mark on this world with pride, knowing that they came from me. They were birthed through me.

Not by the traditional sense, but birthed nonetheless. I stand firm in that – they will be alive in their love and in their purpose.

This gets to be my version, a powerful reclamation of what the path ahead may hold. It is entirely my own. When I tune into my heart, I feel how much I have to give, and how much space there is to take. The many I can show up for in service, and the many creative projects to bring into the world. This creative portal exists within me always, and it is time to start trusting the sacredness of my path because nothing is coincidental, nothing is by accident. No matter where we find ourselves, the twists and turns of the paths ahead, none of that should ever deter us from the value we hold. We are and always have been enough. We have our roles to play in this world. We have space to expand our unique energy and allow it to leave its lasting impression. That imprint is our legacy, and it is already a work in progress.

I honour the women who fall into, choose, embrace, love, struggle with, are exhausted by, and are grateful to be gifted the role of physical mother to the souls who walk earthside and those who guard over us from above.

I honour those who are childless by choice because that choice is sacred, it is sovereign, and entirely your own.

I honour those who are childless not by choice but by circumstance – I witness the ache you hold and the way your love is boundless.

I honour the women in constant motion of redefining themselves and their paths.

All of you. Your place in this world is necessary, needed.

Together, we become the village.

I return complete now, the ribbons dispersing like mist. She is here. Watching, a slightly raised brow, a gentle smile. She gestures for me to look around. To the cards and scribbled drawings on the fridge, to the many painted canvases from my kin's children that are proudly displayed. She directs my gaze to the toy basket overflowing with instruments, books, blocks, the small train that is lodged underneath the lounge, and the handprints smeared across what were once sparkling windows. Childless surrounded by children, bursting with the archetypal energy of creation to birth, nourish, and nurture. I am and always will be a vessel for creation. The more I pour, the more I receive. The perfect garden. Forever cycling through death and rebirth – a never-ending gift.

DANIELLA LIBRI ELIAS is a Cyclic Educator and Coach who has supported hundreds of women in reconnecting to the wisdom they hold within. Guided by her passion for the unique rhythms of our cyclic nature, she feels most at home holding women's circles, meditations, and creative containers. For over a decade, she has poured her energy into the community that surrounds her and is adamant that the women in her spaces are simply sisters meeting on fertile ground. Daniella lives in Sydney in her fairy-light filled home, happiest with a book in one hand and cacao in the other.

@thedaniellaelias | daniellaelias.com

INDIA: THE GREAT SURRENDER

ROSE MASCARO

One week before we went to India, my GP slid a script for antibiotics across the desk. 'You'll need to *surrender* if it happens. Find a local doctor.'

'Surrender?' I scoffed to Jack over dinner, gulping back a little too much wine. 'What kind of advice is that?'

'India will be fine,' he said, patting me on the head with a smirk right up until we landed a week later amongst the sirens and smog of Mumbai city. We shielded ourselves from the dusty glare and the sea of eyes and the shouts of 'Taxi, Taxi!'

When it comes to travel, I've always thrived – and so does Jack, my partner whom I met in the Andes of Peru some years earlier. Cradling steaming cups of coca leaf tea, we'd bonded over high-altitude hiking stories. There's something so electric, so intoxicating, about the thrill of a new land. The freedom to be whoever you want to be.

But India doesn't let you pretend for long. Before we'd even made it out of the airport we'd been scammed at the ATM and hustled a long way in the wrong direction. Finally outside, we tucked our heads down against the crowd of taxi drivers and pulled our backpacks on tight, hoping we didn't look like foreigners. But we were. And so we ended up getting badly ripped off.

Now Jack was in a bad mood with India.

Surrender, I whispered.

To him, or to myself – I'm not sure.

We soon found our way to postcard-worthy paradise in Palolem Beach, Goa. It was everything we could dream of for a holiday: wide beaches, cool bars, cold beers, fresh fish. *Ah, yes – we can surrender here*, we laughed.

On New Year's Eve we feasted on a seafood platter, licking fingers and savouring all we could from every shell and spoon. With bellies full and hearts cracked open, we followed the Goan trance beats across beach bars, dancing under fairy lights with dreadlocked strangers round and round and smiling so hard it felt like our faces might fall apart.

We climbed back into our hotel bed with sand still on our feet. We were madly in love, and we madly loved India. We just had to give it a chance. *Surrender*, we laughed, as we fell asleep to fireworks and a frenzy of barking dogs.

Cheers to the start of a brand new year.

And then our tummies rumbled. Mine first, then Jack's.

By the fourth day, I looked like I might not make it out of India. Jack, pale and hollow-eyed, somehow got us into a rickshaw. The driver, grinning through black teeth, assured us he knew 'the best doctor in India.'

'Surrender,' I whispered to Jack, who was trying not to vomit into his lap.

The driver veered into an unmarked street, past a shoeless man sleeping beside an ATM. No doctor's sign, just a crumbling bakery and a staircase. He pointed up to the second floor.

The steps were grey and grimy, but the doorway at the top glowed:

a red mat, fresh flowers, incense wafting in quiet spirals. Three pairs of shoes were neatly lined outside. I felt annoyed: I've never had to take shoes off to go to the doctor. I placed one foot inside the door like a petulant teenager but a lady with long black hair pointed at my shoes.

I huffed, took them off, and whispered to Jack, 'I'll be pissed if someone steals them.'

Jack kicked off his K-Mart thongs. 'They can take these if they want.'

Inside, the floor was immaculately clean. I sat on a white plastic chair, my bare feet grazing back and forth on the cool shiny tiles. The lady smiled.

The doctor asked two questions, poked my belly twice, and scribbled a prescription while the next patient hovered in the doorway. He charged us six dollars.

And whatever he gave us, worked.

~

Once we were both better, Jack wanted to hire a motorbike. It was his dream to get a 'Royal Enfield' and see the Indian countryside, wind in our hair, 'just like the guy did in *Shantaram*'. Jack found the perfect bike after asking one guy in the markets who led us to another guy who then led us down an alleyway, fingers beckoning, and into the garage of another guy with a big round belly and gold teeth. His name was Wilson. He pointed to a silver bike. It was shiny and fairly new.

Jack beamed. 'This is the one,' he breathed, stroking the chrome of the Enfield like a teenager purchasing his first car. It was so big I wondered if I could get my leg over it. I asked Wilson how safe it was.

Of course, everyone in India tells you everything is *good, good, safe, safe*, especially when it's *cheap, cheap*. Fear curled around my heart as I eased onto the backseat of the bike and grabbed Jack's waist.

He took the handlebars and accelerated, his woman straddled behind him, her long hair gliding luxuriously in the fresh tropical wind. The reality was that the air was not fresh. 'Air quality hazardous', the weather report said each day, and proof was in the smog that lingered like fluffy grey cats wrapping their tails around every skyline. The sheer number of people in India – Mumbai itself teeming with over 20 million, which is almost the entire population of Australia – tells you that there is no simple solution.

As we rode up the winding mountains, I clutched Jack's flesh with each sharp turn. Families in rickshaws stared. Drivers cut past with loud honks. I didn't want to die this way in India.

But soon we found our way to long open country roads framed by impossibly green paddy fields. Long-limbed grandfather trees swayed serenely in the jungle. A monkey sat on a fence and stared at us and I couldn't help but wave with a giggle. Finally, as though reading my mind, Jack pulled into a limestone driveway with a sign saying: 'Spice Farm'.

We swaggered off the bike, our butts relieved as we were handed a lemongrass tea and ushered for a tour around the farm. Our guide taught us about the origins of each plant while we sniffed all the spices of India in their freshest form: pepper, cardamom, cinnamon bark like curled secrets. Lunch was a delicious organic spread of fresh chapati, dal, salads, watermelon. Afterwards, we found waterfalls nearby and took a hike and a swim. The fear fell away as we played in the fresh pools. It was nice, surrendering to all this.

Back on the bike and hugging Jack close, I realised this was actually one of the few times in my life that I had completely surrendered to anyone or anything with so much trust. I started to love the idea of surrender. I loved the exquisite freedom that came with it. With someone else steering for once, my heart spilled over with unconditional love as I fully fell into the richness of the moment.

But as sunset neared, our butts hurting and our eyes savagely windburned, we were grateful to return the bike to its garage. I touched the silver steel one last time and thanked gold-toothed Wilson. 'Come back anytime,' he said, beaming.

That night we found a bright restaurant down the road with mandalas lining the walls and cumin decorating the air. Within minutes of ordering, beaming waiters laid before us half a dozen bubbling magical concoctions tossed with spices and drizzled with cashews and paneer. We ate and ate until our spoons clattered with finality against our fully-scraped plates. *Dessert? Gulab jamun? Sure.* Not only was I still alive, but I was feeling more alive. Over spoonfuls of milky sweetdough we talked about all the things we had seen that day on our motorcycle, ending with a magical sunset that lit up against a rice paddy field. Jack doesn't usually like being photographed, but while staring into the bronze-sky that evening, he'd asked me to take out the camera.

We'd better explore this whole country while we have the chance, we said, delirious on the high of these magical lands and its people. On a whim, we booked a flight the next day to the north. Everything was now moving faster, sharper, brighter.

I sat in the vinyl plane seat, clipped my belt, and smiled to myself. I remembered my first flight as a child – ears hurting, terrifying engines stealing us into the clouds. Hundreds of flights later my fear was now replaced with awe. I held Jack's hand, my co-pilot in life, and smiled as we ascended into smog-stained skies.

~

We arrived in Rishikesh, the spiritual town on the Ganges River, nestled in the foothills of the Himalayas. Flinging our backpacks onto the hotel bed, we caught a free ride into town – and within dizzying seconds of landing on the street, we accepted the first cup of chai tea offered to us. Liquid bubbled on a tiny stovetop before the street vendor poured the creamy brown chai into a handmade clay cup. We held the cups like delicate kittens, the steaming aroma rich with ginger, cardamom, and something I couldn't quite place. We'd forgotten about stomach bugs and slurped loudly, famished for new flavours.

It cost twenty cents.

Somewhere nearby a soft thread of pan flute drifted through the streets. The Ganga Aarti was beginning – the fire ceremony at sunset. Someone handed us a marigold and a candle and gestured for us to remove our shoes.

We stepped barefoot towards the banks of the river, the sky behind the mountains now ablaze in amber and rose. A row of Hindu priests stood like statues, holding high golden lamps that bled light into the dusk. Their chants poured out in rhythmic waves, flowers arcing through the air and kissing the water.

Jack smiled at me, no longer suspicious of everything religious. He was the first to throw his flower in the river. Suddenly we were signing up for everything Rishikesh had to offer – temples, ashtanga yoga, white water rafting, bungee jumping.

~

I stayed upbeat about our decision to jump head first into the Ganges River until I was at the very edge of the bungee platform. Panic struck, hard, when I saw there was no water to break the fall: the riverbed below was all teeth and rock.

Three, two, one! I didn't hesitate when they told me to jump; there was no point. I launched into a dive and a death-cry that echoed throughout the valleys of the Ganges.

You look back at your life and you realise that you never want to die.

You love your life. You love who you are.

You are falling to your death.

And then –

Then you come back to life, better than ever.

You bounce, and each time you scream, but now with a giggle. Now you can see where you are; etched rockfaces, blue streams, clouds above. 'Wow!' You are being lowered toward two smiling men and you're so delirious you might actually be dribbling on them upside-down. Your eyes are watering and your head feels like it's exploded. No – you were probably just screaming too much.

And you talk like a drug addict to these two guys who unharness you – 'Oh that's why the bungee is not set up on water!' – you babble. They smile as they unstrap you and hand you a bottle of water. Something to drink, something to hold. They point 'over there' and you drunk-stumble across a trickling stream towards a group of people, those who had just completed the jump before you. They have hands on hips, squinting at the bungee tower. It takes you forever to navigate across the rocks. Like a baby calf, you think to yourself. You eventually make it. 'You did a really nice dive,' they say. You feel proud that you had a good technique for the end of your life. The adrenaline is real.

~

From the bottom of the riverbed, I tipped my head up and saw Jack on the platform. And I knew for sure that he was going to be OK. I got over my fear of dying in the space of three minutes and now I felt love for everything in a way I'd never loved before. Even myself.

Jack handled the fear of death way better than me. After his first shouts of joy, he seemed almost bored. 'It was over too fast,' he shrugged, ready for his next activity. He's really good at chasing thrills, but terrible at sitting still.

~

Our first Indian yoga class was held on a cold marble floor. We were early to class, and we were the only ones there: seated cross-legged in front of our tiny teacher who stared at us with large white eyes. He was so thin, I wondered if they paid him enough to eat. He looked up at the clock. We looked up at the clock. The Himalayan winter chill permeated through my worn-out yoga mat and I shivered.

I figured I would pretend to meditate. I closed my eyes for a few seconds, then opened them slightly and peered to the left to check what Jack was doing. He was doing the same, but with a frown.

Soon class began with a tiny teacher instructing us to take huge breaths in terrible English. Despite the rocky start, he moved with grace and intuition, and we followed. 'Breathe innnnnnn. Breathe outtttttttt.' As he gained confidence with his English instructions, he moved around the room and adjusted us. We couldn't help but surrender to his bony, all-knowing hands. Before we knew it, we came to inversions – the tricky 'upside down' part of the class.

Despite Jack's reckless nature, he refused. 'I don't do headstands.' The teacher whispered something in Jack's ear. Jack nodded. I turned away for one second – and suddenly Jack flipped into a perfect head-stand. 'Yes, yes, and now you are in the King position of yoga,' the teacher whispered. I ran for my bag and grabbed the camera. The teacher stood next to Jack and faced the camera, holding one of Jack's legs. His forehead only came up to Jack's knees.

I showed Jack the photo later: It looked like an ancient, grainy photo, like one of Iyengar's early days of teaching. Even though the teacher wasn't smiling, he looked proud.

Jack laughed. He was lightheaded, delirious, a little like me coming off the bungee. 'I didn't think I could do that, honestly,' Jack breathed. The tiny teacher smiled.

'The body is strong but the mind is weak.' He reached up and squeezed Jack's arm, at least three times the size of his own.

'If the mind has no fear, the body can do anything.'

~

From Rishikesh we braided our way east and west: Taj Mahal's achingly beautiful symmetry; Pushkar's famous holy lake; the pink city of Jaipur; the kite festival stitching multicolours into wintery sky. A night bus to Jaisalmer desert took us to the golden fort which shone like a fairytale. We rode a motorcycle one last time here: I asked to. This time I loved every second, my smile effervescent and my long hair trailing through the desert.

Perhaps our teacher was right: it is only the mind that is our weakness. I realised I'm not afraid of death – I'm afraid of discomfort. We have everything we could possibly want at home in Australia, and somehow I'm always fragile, sick, tired, making excuses. Unable to step outside my comfort zone. But here, discomfort is like a mantra, a way of life that brings infinite possibility and peace. The ancient Sanskrit word, *Santosha,* means embracing all aspects of life – to feel a deep sense of inner contentment. And my favourite word I learned, *Ananda*: a deep, unshakeable sense of bliss.

A woman passed us with bags of groceries balanced like grace.

'Namaste,' she said with a smile. *The light in me greets the light in you.* It is both a greeting and instruction. Look for the light. Bow to it. Become it.

~

Once I lost the fear, I saw everything more clearly. Doorways bloomed with bright flowers and incense, noisy streets filled with unconditional love. We kicked off our dirty shoes without complaint, wrapped ourselves in scarves and bindis, and ate delicious thali filled with Ayurvedic nutrition and good karma. Sitting at a rooftop restaurant under the stars with a feast, we'd delight in the funny and inspiring stories of the people that we met that day. No wifi, no devices – just us. Jack and I spent the most quality time together that we'd ever had; we'd never talked or laughed so much.

There are so many other stories: the hordes of locals entranced by Jack's luminous skin; the camaraderie of cows who destroyed shopfronts when snacks appeared; angry shopkeepers swatting them away – abandoning sacred Hinduism in the protection of business; riding camels in the rolling dunes of the desert at sunset; eating crunchy curry cooked during a sandstorm; the hotel manager who shared in vivid detail his excitement about his upcoming arranged marriage; the quiet miracle of waking up each morning with wonder in the room. The list goes on, as it does with places that rewire you.

~

The day after we got back home to overly-perfect Australia, with its clean horizon and crossword-like streets, my thongs were stolen at the beach. The same flip-flops I'd worn all through India, left at every doorway. I laughed. I didn't need them.

We'd got used to bare feet. We'd got used to feeling dusty, and the sounds of laughing Indian men and chanting music at 4.30 a.m. and screaming motorbikes and monkeys that stole fruit. We'd got used to all of it, and somehow it made us better people.

Salty and barefoot, we walked down the street, Jack dripping and refreshed, me dripping with the colourful fabrics and jewels of India.

We smiled at everyone.

They stared.

But after a few moments, they couldn't help but surrender to our smiles.

Namaste.
I see and honour the light in you.

ROSE MASCARO is an Australian writer, editor and teacher who is passionate about teaching others how to connect with their most authentic, heart-led words. She's the former editor of Teen Breathe magazine, Australia's leading mindfulness magazine for teens, and holds a master's degree in creative writing from UTS, Sydney. In 2020 Rose launched HeartWriting® Australia where she teaches powerful, authentic writing from the heart using a combination of literature, meditation, spirituality, heart theory, and creative psychology. Her sellout writing workshops and retreats are a perfect blend of spiritual connection and writing technique. Rose has authored two books, is published in magazines and anthologies internationally, and has co-authored a range of Australian titles.

The Heart Writing Handbook: A journey into the magic of heart-led writing and storytelling (available now).

@heartwriting.com.au

THE STORIES WE TELL

BENITA BENSCH

For my greatest teachers and living masterpieces
Bruce, Bronson, Myles and Lawson

It's a Saturday afternoon and the Take Forty Australia countdown is playing on the beloved double cassette deck in my lap. I'm sitting on the grass outside to minimise the chance of being interrupted mid-taping. Like other music-loving children of the 80s, it's my favourite time of the week, when I get to immerse myself in the new and rising hits and tape my favourites to savour until next weekend.

I'm working on perfecting my timing to hit record in the split second between the host's introduction finishing and the next track starting, so as to capture it whole and pristine. I have to be choosy about what I record, and where, because I have only a few well-worn cassettes I can use for taping.

The mix tapes I make each week are the soundtrack of my life, an expression of who I am. I exist to their rhythm – my constant companion in moments of joy, anxiety and fear. At times, the music notes make it into my feet and they jiggle without me realising. I'm the kid who lives for school discos and Christmas concerts, and I dream of singing and dancing when I'm a grown-up.

I never follow that desire, though, because that world seems so far removed from my daily life and the seriousness of my nature. It's something only other people would do – people who are not me.

~

It's big lunch on a Wednesday and I'm perched in front of the box-like computer located near the windows at one end of my primary school classroom. It's the first and only one for our sixteen or so students and the only computer in my life. When I print, I secretly get a kick out of tearing off the perforated sprocket hole edges. It feels so productive and professional – like something someone in an office would do. However, I'm not drawn to this novel thing with its green screen and block letters for its technological capabilities; rather, for the promise of a vehicle to convert the idea in my mind to a form I can hold in my hands.

I'm creating a real-life book. It's a guinea pig reference book complete with text, photographs and hand-drawn pictures, to describe their hair types, coat colours, diet, care needs, breeding habits, and very importantly, how to accurately distinguish between the sexes. The completed pages feel crisp, precious, and bumpy on the back where the photos are glued on. I try hard to keep them organised and in perfect condition, setting the goal then and there to publish a proper book when I'm old enough.

I love immersing myself in a good project. The excitement that ripples through me drives me to work on it in whatever spare time I can find at home and school. I'm enthralled, determined. It's my private indulgence, but it's also for other serious guinea-pig-breeder kids like me who absolutely *must* read it.

However, in time, I tuck it away in my camphor chest where I keep all my special trinkets: my diaries, a postcard, pen pal letters, a few red and green ribbons, an Expo '88 stamped coin, and now, a guinea pig book.

~

It's a Monday night and I'm curled up on my single bed with my diary and scrapbook. It's where I know myself best, where I escape to the cocoon of my thoughts. I feel so lucky to have, in my opinion, the best kids' bedroom in our house. More often than not, I have both doors shut so I can play music of my choosing and drift off into a joy-filled bubble of expression. I fill the journal with poems, quotes and song lyrics that lure me toward them. Words captivate me, and I wonder if I'm weird.

I write in my diary almost daily and love to cut out pictures from magazines, greeting cards, and Reader's Digest books to glue them into the scrapbook. I do a lot of doodling, draw love hearts and daydream about people, animals and places.

These rituals fill my heart, but I have an ever-present fear that someone will discover my latest crush and read my deepest thoughts on these pages. For this reason, I keep them hidden away under lock and key.

~

It's 10.30 am on a Friday in August 2024 and my hands are wet with clay. I'm seated with nine other women at a long table, and as I scan their faces, I see in their expressions what it means to reclaim your spark. More than that, I *feel* what it means. There's an energy present that's challenging to articulate – perhaps described as a collective release, concurrent with an expansion of possibility. I'm riding its wave, and I sense I'm not the only one.

In this moment, I'm reminded again how it feels to create; to convert the idea in my mind to a form I can hold in my hands. It's spectacular. I close my eyes and remember.

~

In the space between, the little version of me who delighted in illustrating her creations was replaced by the version who wouldn't touch a coloured pencil to paper unless there were lines to stay within. The last time I felt good about freehand drawing was winning a ribbon at our local show for an Anzac Day picture I did at school. Beyond that, I stuck to scribbling flowers, lines and shapes for their ease, structure and predictability. Patterns felt safer in my body. I think I unconsciously compared myself to a more artistic figure in my life and concluded that if I couldn't draw really well – better than her – then I wouldn't even try. *You're just not good enough.*

Even when I still liked being 'crafty', I began to prefer guide rails so that I knew things were going to turn out. I kept to cross-stitch sets with instructions and paint-by-number kits with clear outcomes. *There's a right way and a wrong way, and getting it right is the best way.*

Words came more naturally to me – numbers too – and I was recognised for my ability with numbers, so that seed was planted and watered with praise and glowing report cards. Words and numbers have rules and formulas, so I knew when I was doing them right and well. I liked that. You're rewarded and smiled at more when you do it right and well. Is it any wonder that I invisibly, yet definitively, morphed from a fluid, singing, dancing little being into something more rigid? *It feels better inside if you be good and do good.*

I felt a pang in grade ten when my friends, beaming, would show me the incredible creations they'd made in art. I could see *them* in their work, so expressive, so alive, like personality made visible. I wanted my school subjects to have such zest. Instead, I felt less-than with my very sensible, relatively lifeless subjects that I excelled at but never felt pride in unless I was winning an award. At the time, I couldn't put my finger on what felt like a persistent negative undertow. I wanted the courage they possessed, that for some reason

I didn't have anymore, to freely create. *How are they so creative? How do they know what to do?*

What story had they been told that I hadn't? On reflection, I suspect it didn't unfold so literally. Though I can't recall it being a conscious decision, the *I'm not good at art* thought became an *I'm not creative* conscious story. With time, that story became the embedded subconscious story: *I'm not a creative person*. Then, with repetition, that story became part of my belief system and who I thought I was. Or rather, summed up who I was *not*.

Society, with all its expectations and ideals, had gotten its hands on me – the highly sensitive, intuitive, friendly, often anxious, guinea-pig-loving girl – and was teaching me who I was supposed to be.

By my senior years, I was akin to a studious robot, studying two kinds of maths and multiple science subjects as prerequisites to a veterinary science degree. I later chose rural science instead, which funnelled me into university subjects including biochemistry, statistics, plant and animal science. *I'm good at this, so I must be on the right track.*

My results thrived because facts made sense, and my photographic memory served me well. Had I been called to actually apply my knowledge I may not have really *known* the material, but I had a great system in place for memory and short-term recall. There was also sport, partying, an international exchange, then an honours year and early career in agriculture with more science, data and technology. *Pursuing, striving, achieving – that's just what I do.*

While getting on with life, my sorely neglected hyper-coloured inner world contracted so gradually that even I didn't notice it. The seduction of achievement – to do right and well – led me to more 'sturdy' life path choices and away from what I perceived as whimsical. I couldn't be one of those dreamer types – I'd somehow concluded there's no place for dreamers or artists in the world of success. There's a lot to prove if you want to be good enough. *It hurts too much when you try and fail.*

I maintained my warm, bubbly personality, and in time there was a level of creativity in my work and my kitchen, but I couldn't bring myself to simply play or create uninhibitedly. In real time, I didn't even know it was missing. Life was full of big adult responsibilities – building businesses, wealth and a family – and if you're not good at art, you're not creative anyway, right? You're meant to focus and get ahead when you're young, so I thought. There's no value in fluffing about, even when mental illness grabs hold of you from time to time. *I'm just prone to stress.*

With mothering four children four and under, time for myself was a rarity, let alone time for creativity. What were my interests anymore anyway? What would I create even if I had the time? I was terrified of the blank canvases I occasionally bought the kids to paint on. The clean sheets of butcher's paper in the playroom were as inviting as they were a sure path to self-disappointment. I felt the odd glimmer in my brief interludes with blocks and glitter, but it was fleeting and foreign. There were always more pressing things to do. *Must keep moving.*

We are all innately creative. These were the words that, in 2018, changed my perspective, and ultimately the trajectory of my creative life. *What? Really?* Over time I attracted more learnings to this effect that reaffirmed this concept and presented me with a compelling new story to replace the engrained *I'm not creative* one. It's not that some of us are magically endowed with creativity while others are not; everyone is creative. *We are all creative.*

I heard these words for the first time – or was ready to hear them for the first time – in a coaching program I'd enrolled in to find some semblance of self in the fog of early motherhood. I was thirty-seven, feeling lost, heavy with obligation, consumed by anxiety and a shame tucked down deep in the maternity pants covering a postnatal body that didn't feel like mine. Through this program, I set myself the only big goal I'd set in years that wasn't business or family focused. It scared, stretched and excited me in a way I hadn't felt since the guinea pig project: I was going to write my first grown-up book. *But how do you think you're going to do it, Benita?*

The idea of it had been niggling at me for years. I'd kept a journal through our years of trying to conceive and wanted to collate and share the journal entries in a way that would support other women on the often-treacherous fertility journey. I'd previously dismissed the idea with every possible reason I could channel, but it just wouldn't go away. When the stretch goal section of the coaching program sat before me, it was the most meaningful item on my 'wants' list. This whisper from my soul was such that I didn't really have a choice in the matter. It felt like the time, though I had no idea how or when I was going to accomplish it. My coach encouraged me to make the committed decision anyway. *Jump and you'll grow wings.*

The fears showed up one by one, again and again. The limiting beliefs came to visit too, trying to keep me safe. *You don't know how to write a book. Who's going to read it? You're not a writer. Who do you think you are? You should be doing something that earns money.* On many occasions, I sat at our dining room table with my head in my hands, finding the strength to overcome my harsh inner voices by returning to the screen and typing just one more word, sentence, paragraph. I built confidence through taking action. Initially, it was incredibly difficult to prioritise even five minutes of writing time, but it became easier as I gained momentum and shifted my internal narrative from *I should be working* to *this is important work too.* I even hired extra help to give me space for it, which was a huge breakthrough for me at the time.

Returning to writing was the spark that rekindled my inner flame which had felt snuffed out for a very long time. I loved being a mum, and I was happy with my life, but deep down I felt stagnant – withered – and until then I hadn't been able to figure out why. With a jolt, it dawned on me one day: writing is *my* creativity! I remember now; *this* is what lights me up! As I began shifting the inner story, adjusting my daily priorities and habits, my book – *The Art of Trying* – became a living, breathing thing in our home. Being in that beautiful creative state put me in a high vibration that permeated every area of my life. I promised myself never to forget again. *I feel alive.*

A few years later, a friend invited me to join her for a Paint 'n Sip session happening thirty kilometres away in our small rural community. I'd already seen it advertised, basically glazed over it and tried to ignore the fact it was on. The old voice had reared its ugly head again. *Remember you're not artistic, Benita. Writing is one thing, this is another.* My friend persisted, and because we hadn't caught up in a while, I convinced myself it was a great opportunity to spend some time together. I begrudgingly agreed. *You've got this, Benita. It's not a contest.*

I was surprised by how much fun it actually was. Did the not-enough thoughts and moments of perfectionist paralysis surface? You bet they did, with a vengeance. But as we all chatted, caffeinated, painted and laughed, I realised I was the only one who cared about my cow painting. No one was watching, scoring or judging me – only myself. It was me versus me in my ongoing wrestle with self-imposed expectations. I looked around the room, exhaled just a little, let go just a notch. My heart swells when I see my painting and recall the joy-filled morning that it was. *Maybe this is what life is all about.*

While at this event, I overheard someone say, 'I haven't got a creative bone in my body.' I inwardly winced at the pain the familiarity of the phrase evoked in me. The very same had left my own lips innumerable times over decades. What a loss the *I'm not a creative person* limiting belief would prove to be, depriving me of countless opportunities for joy because I was too afraid of looking foolish and not being able to do it, or heaven forbid, not get it right. How sad that I would hold myself back because not trying felt safer than getting it wrong. Though I try to live without regret, I quietly grieve for the rich experiences I avoided in adulthood because this belief defined the boundaries of my life. All those times I said no instead of yes. All those times I didn't believe in myself for fear of being exposed. I suppose, however, without the lesson I wouldn't have the learning. *It's OK to be vulnerable.*

A woman's creative life is a glorious, sacred thing. At times, I've only glimpsed it through a keyhole into others' lives. At times, I've experienced its full power in my own, like when I started my first ever singing lessons at age forty-two. Creativity gives us a way to express ourselves, to heal, to find meaning in a world that so often asks so much without always giving back. Whether it's writing, pottery, art, music, craft, gardening, cooking, weaving, sewing, dancing, sweeping, or making, our creativity lets us reclaim our stories, be who we are and reimagine new ways of being, not just for ourselves, but for the people around us. This is important work. When we nurture our creativity, we're nourishing something deep, and we're creating space to simply be – fully, freely, seen as we are. It offers us a lifelong playground in which to play, and to learn something new about ourselves as we draw on our essence to inform our next expression of self. *To create is to grow.*

In my mothering and work, I'm often reminded of this, including in 2024 when co-hosting a women's retreat centred around creative expression. Oh, the irony. I faced my fear of a blank canvas by plastering it in paint pens, stickers, and words. *Don't think, just do, Benita.* It was insanely fulfilling. A magical energy filled the room as our group made pottery together – our hearts and hands moulding clay in individual, wondrous ways as we connected on a frequency of creation. There is something very beautiful about taking an idea and giving it form in the physical realm, multiplied by the energetic frequency of the collective. *This is how we're designed to be: creating, connected.*

Creative expression in whatever form feels good should not be perceived as a luxury. It is essential. If we don't express our creativity, we suppress it, and that suppressed energy manifests in low-vibration emotion stored in our body. I often observe women, me included, only *allowing* ourselves a dose of creativity once the work is done. It reminds me of how society conditions us: be a good little girl and then you'll get a sticker. I'm no longer waiting for a sticker from anyone. What I've found to be true is that if I do the reverse – embrace my creativity first – the work that follows is more joyful and effortless. It raises my energetic vibration and connects me to my true authentic self, such that whatever follows can't help but be raised too. *You have permission.*

We are designed to create. We create through our original thoughts in every moment and, additionally, we each have talents and abilities that we express in different ways. We always have access to our creativity through our imagination – one of the mental faculties we, as humans, are blessed with. What a precious gift to explore.

~

I tell the little girl:
She is amazing, safe, enough.
To keep dancing, singing to the cows and into her hairbrush.
To embrace her writing and share it with the world.
She can't fail. There's only learning.
To create and play just for fun, and follow what brings her joy no matter what the world says or thinks.
The whole point is the journey, not the destination.
No matter what path she takes she'll come back to herself.
It's time for forgiveness.
I hold her and promise I'll tell her future children what she wants them to know: You *are* creative – brilliantly, in full colour, without even trying. *I see you.*

BENITA BENSCH is a writer, coach, speaker, farmer and mum of four living near Moama, NSW. She helps women evolve from feeling invisible to seen again, guiding them to reclaim their spark, clarity, wellbeing, and a life shaped from within. Author of The Art of Trying and a certified Motherhood Studies Practitioner, Benita draws on her background in marketing, agriculture, and personal development. She believes in the power of storytelling to connect, heal and illuminate. Her second book, published in 2026, explores the journey to one's true self through the light and dark of motherhood.

Visit Benita at www.benitabensch.com and
@benitabensch on Instagram, Facebook, LinkedIn.

WANT

COURTNEY ZERAFA

'We pretend to want things we don't want so nobody can see us not getting what we need.'
—Lisa Taddeo, Three Women

An advertisement pops up on my Instagram feed. There is a machine they can zap over your thighs to smooth out cellulite ridden skin into a smooth fortress, like a newborn baby who is fresh from the womb; like a newborn baby who has not yet tasted life, or worried about the bills, or put a swimsuit over their sweating flesh.

I click the link, curious. For two hundred dollars, they will zap my skin for an hour. In as many as four sessions, you can start to see improvements. It will take time, is the insinuation. Further than this: you have lived with your skin as it is for your entire life up until this point, what is four sessions in the scheme of things?

I close the browser but from that point on I am already doomed. AI has calculated my next steps. It has furrowed into my brain now and it intends to furrow even deeper. Each time I scroll, there will be a new advertisement. I've already thought about it once, dipped my toes into the abyss; I've already positioned myself as the deer, ready to be hunted by lions. I have laid my bare stomach for fresh teeth to sink into. As is the way with capitalism, and patriarchy, and the overarching sense that there is always something about ourselves we can hone and perfect.

Next come the advertisements for micro-needling, and derm-abrasion, and a machine you can purchase and use at home to clear out the wrinkles from your laugh lines. The age of wellness, for a woman, is the era of preserving as much youth as possible. The highest bidder wins. The latest technologies snatch away self-esteem. Your lips could be a little more plump, surely. Your nose, obviously too crooked. Your skin sags when you hit thirty, that's what they tell you. Your body is producing less collagen so you must supplement, enhance, rectify before it is too late and you are sitting with aching skin that can no longer be modified to perfection.

When I am 25 I wear a pale blue dress to work that hugs my skin. My frame is obvious, my hips wide, my stomach acceptable. A colleague who is teetering on 32 looks me over. Her smile is curt, and behind her glasses her hazel eyes loom.

'Enjoy that body while you have it,'
she says to me, 'soon it will all change.'

It is not a threat, by any means. Rather, a declaration. Our bodies, as with time, wither away. Such is the case of ageing. In a world where the aesthetics of women are commoditised, our beauty is the most fierce weapon in our arsenal.

What is it all *for*, though, I ponder. Do I keep my skin tight in order to ensure I capitalise on my intelligence, to be given a chance to be looked at? The most frightful thing is to be overlooked. To not be spectacular, youthful, enhanced, means risking being hidden, wasting away behind the curtains. If I cannot capture your attention in the first instance, does that mean everything else that is contained within my vessel is never noticed?

In the ice bath, the cold wraps so thoroughly around my arteries that I can feel each shudder of my heart. Its beat is resounding and reminding. I am alive, despite the shrinking of my flesh. I can feel the goosebumps raising as my body sinks closer to death, my heart all the while pumping against the frost, ordering the blood to find my limbs. Despite itself, the body remains breathing.

I pull my body out of the icy water and stretch before entering the sauna. There is a holiness to the practice. My heart rate quickens when my body is burning; I am sweating and yearning and doing breathwork. Then I get back into the ice, my heartbeat slowing down perceptibly, and I feel the opposite.

The first time I did this practice, I felt the closest to peace that I had ever felt. There was nothing to focus on except the functions of my body. The way it fought against the circumstances and remained alive.

This is a practice that is rampant in society today, welcomed by athletes and influencers alike. It is sold in the same vein as wellness, and so is intimately linked to preserving the body by any means. It helps with muscle recovery, mental health; it is sold and weaponised and used as a means to justify why we should keep our bodies, *for a fee*, in their most youthful expression for as long as possible.

As I ease into my ageing, I am finding comfort in the new rises of my flesh. The way my body bends differently, and the strange aches that appear out of nowhere. This body has birthed and loved and danced and will one day turn to ash. This body continues to age, and with each day that passes it sends me small reminders that today I am closer to death than I was yesterday. That each minute holds fervour because each minute could be my last.

When I was 19, I decided my chest was not large enough. There were no dresses that fit both my hips and my breasts. The bras I wore worked as cavities, reminding me that my body, as a woman, was not living up to the hype.

With an inheritance and a naive brain, I booked in for a consultation with a plastic surgeon and had a new chest by the end of the next month. The first thing I remember from those first few weeks with my new chest was this: a sincere and acute knowing that there was a foreignness about my flesh that was like acid burning through everything I had been. I could not drive, could not lift my arms high enough to get to the steering wheel for two weeks; I could not lay on my back and push my body up without someone else pulling my arms. I distinctly recall waking one morning and calling out to my dad from my bedroom, feeling panic, and asking him if he could help me out of bed. When I got home from the surgery, my best friend visited me with a gift: a fire engine red, laced bra.

It has almost been ten years since the surgery, and I know that soon I will need to get them either replaced or removed. They are a foreign object within my body, sewn deep into my chest, a ticking time bomb. They tell you this before you get it done: that the silicone will need replacing at some point. At that point – *ten years down the track* – I would probably have to get bigger implants to account for the stretching of my skin and the withering of the silicone.

When I was 19, the concept of turning 29 seemed incomprehensible. *Of course* I would be ok getting them a larger size by then. I did not think about the future financial implications, health concerns, my body arching in new ways, my mind shifting and metamorphosing and growing from what it once was. I was the deer, dazzled by bright headlights, excited to change my body to become something that I thought I would like more than what I already was.

After about five years of having them inside my skin, I did an internet search to try and decipher why I felt constantly fatigued and vaguely unwell, and the search results displayed a surplus of women who had also had breast implant surgery and reported the same symptoms. I delved deeper and found that when there is a foreign object placed inside your body, whether it be a piercing or silicone implants, the body is *constantly* fighting to get rid of the foreign object. It concentrates on that area because it does not understand what has infiltrated its space, and wants to evacuate it.

It has not all been gloom: I have worn dresses, admired my body in a bikini, enjoyed wearing shirts without the need for a bra. They have garnered an insurmountable amount of pleasure from both me and those who have witnessed them. In many ways, what was once foreign is now familiar to me. I have learned the new rise of my chest in such a way that I can no longer picture what my frame would look like if I did not have them. Over time, my nerves have mended. In the sixth year I could feel fingers running over the skin again. By the time I had my child, I could feel his mouth as he drank milk against my nipple. While there is something within my body that was once not mine, they have still allowed me to nurse my child, suffered the impacts of ageing, and though they are by no means sagging, they have a puckered edge that shows me how they have grown *with* me.

I visit the ice bath and sauna whenever I am seeking peace. It is not a punishment I force my body to endure, but a practice that brings me closer to its functions. Though recently, I learned that because the female and male body is wired so differently, the impacts of an activity such as an ice bath have a different weight for each.

A woman's womb is a sacred place, and it is not supposed to be exposed to such freezing temperatures. It is meant to stay warm, holy.

And it makes me think: the capitalist world feeds off of monetary currency and patriarchal values, and it does not disclose what the cold can do to a woman. It is almost the same as when the male surgeon told me the breast implant procedure was perfectly safe, and that the risks and long-term consequences were minimal.

My 19 year old self was exposed to Snapchat filters: the one that turned you into a puppy, and how Kylie Jenner used it regularly. It smoothed your pores and gave you dog ears; it increased your lip size, decreased your nose size, and let you lick the screen with your puppy tongue. My 19 year old self was exposed to Victoria's Secret models who disclosed their rigorous training schedules and the food they ate in a day: cucumber and carrot sticks with hummus. Boxing, skipping, Pilates. I watched the Australian Open and noted the way the female tennis players had toned thighs, free from puckering flesh, and decided to work out the same ways that they did.

All this does not mean much except for the fact that it shaped my decision to change my body in a huge way. Now, young women are consistently told that they must do everything they can do to stay young. Now, it is marketed in such a way that we are told it is for the *best*. If we want to be healthy, we must visit the gym every day. New proteins hit the market, saunas can detox the weight away, there is a machine that can fix your thighs, a serum you purchase to stop the effects of ageing.

It is *dangerous*, what is sold as health. It is dangerous how accessible it is to skip the impact of time.

It is healthy to nurture your body, to give it good food, to bend your muscles and run. It is healthy to take time to meditate, and swallow vitamins, and replenish your soul by any means necessary. It is *not* healthy to navigate your days doing all you can to impede the way your body naturally morphs.

When I click the advertisements on Instagram, I feel overwhelming insecurity. Of course I want to have smooth skin and a taut frame and a button nose. I want my lips to be kissable, I want cat eyes that are magnetising with lashes to match. I want better posture, tight glutes, arms that do not sag. I want, I want, I want.

I picture myself on a surgeon's table: flesh marked with thick black texters, indicating the parts they would cut off, make smaller, adjust slightly. On this surgeon's table I would lay mute, naked, face covered in a mask. My eyes closed, my soul absent, the room a sterile white. I would smell disinfectant and rubber gloves and there would be scissors laying on the bench that could penetrate my crumbling flesh. Blood would be spilled and it would be crimson against the marble floor. The surgeon would chop away until all that is left is something of a shell. This surgeon might accidentally cut away the tattoo I got when I was 21; his gleaning force would slice right through that poppy flower on my left arm that I got in honour of my grandfather and my arms would be firm. He might smooth out the wrinkles under my eyes with a laser beam, and when I wake I might forget all the glorious nights I spent nursing a newborn. All the time could be ripped from me, and it would be so easy, and it would make me so palatable, so *relevant*, so alluring to upload a selfie of my perfect face to Instagram after I've woken and my surgery scars have faded.

I want, I want, I want and as a woman I will always want. Yet, my greatest hunger sits within sharing a bottle of wine and a pizza with my best friends. It resides in the laugh lines that remind me of that one time I laughed so hard I thought I may never breathe again. It fits inside my hips that are wider now they have pushed a baby out of my womb, and the legs that have carried me through the streets of Notting Hill, and the toes that have touched the sweeping sands of Malibu. My hands that reach and reach and hold. My anger, my fraught desire, my force as a woman that no longer wishes to become a performing act for the male gaze to rest upon. I no longer wish to be seen because I have the straightest teeth. I want to dodge the lions, I want to sift through the years that are eating me alive, and feel awe that I have been granted so much time and that my body wears the weight of every memory.

I do my Pilates, I drink the protein shake. I click the ridiculous advertisements. And each time, I feel as though I have dodged a bullet. Each time I want to change something about my body, I wonder *why* I want. I do not wish to be a newborn baby that is fresh out of the womb, I wish and I want to hold everything dear.

COURTNEY ZERAFA is a freelance writer who lives just outside of Sydney, Australia. When she isn't living out the consequences of her gilded desire, she is tending to her multiple fur babies and human baby. You can spill your heart out to her via Instagram, or you can let her spill her heart out to you on her Substack. @korts

BIBBIDI-BOBBIDI-BOO

COURTNEY ZERAFA

We make the waiting beautiful. We do, don't we? We smash everything else into tiny pieces and we wait on the curbside, or on our couch; we pour a glass of wine and put on Netflix at the end of a long day of chores; we paint the walls pixie pink, we fix our hair, we buy a new pair of shoes; we transform all of this waiting into a holy act.

I tilt my face upwards, toward the golden architraves, and I don't think they've got a good enough photograph of me to hang so high on display. They chose the selfie I had taken the week before I met the prince. True, my eyes do seem relatively bright in it. But if you look closer you can see that my smile is lower on the left side. I didn't notice until now, until this moment when it's all over, that my smile was always muted.

They could've chosen a photo from the night of the ball, that would have made more sense. I was glittering that night, I remember it well. When you are shining so bright, you always do attract the moths. Is it my fault, then, for glistening too loud?

I guess the problem started when I was ignoring, and waiting, and *pining*. It's the only reason I snuck out and put on the fancy dress. It was exhilarating to do something I knew I was not supposed to do. I wanted love, I wanted to *taste* life. I wanted to dance until midnight.

I told my godmother that glass slippers were a bad idea, but she had me squeeze my tiny feet into them anyway.

"Make the most of your beautiful, young, agile body while you can." she had told me with a flick of her wrist.

I do see the logic. Now that everything has dried up, I wish I had danced a little longer and brooded a little less.

I think, for the most part, I made my waiting beautiful. What else was there to do but to romanticise the life of a maid? Piles and piles of laundry, washed and cleaned and washed again. The living room was always spotless, the gardens always neat. I would frolick, as cheesy as it may sound, in between the flowers while I weeded. I would let the kittens run around my feet, and I would listen to the birds as they sang. It was probably insanity, or mania, or loneliness, but I always swore they could understand me better than any human could.

Weeding is harder than you think, too. Pulling roots from hardened soil takes true bicep strength. Sometimes they burrow so far beneath the Earth it knocks you backwards to pull them out. Dirt under my finger nails, grubby toes, hair that was knotted from too much grease. But the sunlight hitting the wisps of my hair gave it a golden tone, and it felt like a halo.

Yet, I was always waiting for something bigger and better and mightier to sweep me off my feet. The irony of it all is hilarious.

Perhaps there is a part of me that wishes that there had been someone taking secret photographs of me while I pined my days away. It would have been more accurate to hoist a photo of me high above all these people that showed me dirty: in my apron, over the boiling pot while I made soup, sleeping on the worn down mattress. I crave honesty now that the performance is over, and yet it seems like everyone else is hellbent on maintaining this ghastly falsity.

Cinderella ran too fast up the stairs, said the newspaper clipping.

Away, away, away from the chasing man, is the part they left out.

I think what I clasped onto most tight during all those years of waiting was hope. Not hope as this holy thing, but hope as this fragile bird, flapping its flailing wing while clinging to a breaking branch. And then the daylight bleaches the Earth and the branch snaps. Who can hear it when the bird falls to the ground?

Tell me, and please grant me your honesty, isn't hope the tactical response to unmatched grief? And isn't unmatched grief the place where all of our misplaced love goes to rest? Tell me, aren't our fingers constantly reaching into the ghostlike air for *anything* until we find *something* to pull us back? Until the desperation that puts sauce over our heart gets so sickly sweet that it bleeds acrid and we are forced to bend our desire to the whims of whichever hand is reaching back.

I think about that most of all now, while I hover above all these people. The venue is lovely: rows of lacquered, wooden pews, stained glass windows, intricate, brilliant carvings springing from the ceiling. There are white candles burning beneath me, held upright by polished brass candlesticks. All this misplaced love and unmatched grief. I could touch the flame right now and it would not burn me.

I am not cynical, and I am not sad, please don't get me wrong. I am just reminiscing.

Maybe I did run too fast up the stairs. The stairs were steep, and they were garnished with a sleek, slim, red carpet that hid the sharp granite beneath. Everything dangerous is always covered over with red, so I should've known.

Even while I donned an apron, I've always been dramatic. Life is too short not to be, isn't it? The whole debacle of living needs livening up. So I put on my best jewels, I wore the dress that shimmered under the strobe lights, because I wanted a night *off*. Part of my waiting was having that night off.

A ghastly trip, was the pun the newspapers used. It did make me cringe, reading it. But I suppose it was. *Ghastly,* that is.

Of course I caught the attention of the prince. It wasn't what I had intended to do, but as I said, moths to a flame. And while it lasted, it was beautiful. And now the grieving is twofold; I do not wish to hold his hand again, that's not what this grieving is – I was running *away* from him, afterall – but it would be nice to feel something solid under my fingertips again.

I remember it quite specifically, lucidly, and I expect that is how most final moments go. We had rushed outside, into the cool air, hands woven together, away from the loud music. My dress was tangled from running and that should have been warning enough. Then, under a giant sycamore we slowed down. My breath eased. I recall the quiet, the still, the fireflies dancing around my face. Were they real or am I placing them there now? How much of our memory is simply longing? I can feel my hand sitting on his chest, his fingers on my lower back. I can hear his laugh, and then I can hear it turning jagged, pleading, rough.

This isn't about the prince, so how long are we allowed to grieve for? If the love is alive and bursting but has no place to go, for how long do we continue to dance the dance? And which fickle human emotion keeps us trapped in this sacred embrace? The ego with its banging fist as it screams, "*you must not be the one to accept defeat!*"? The desire with its soft glow, "*just hold me a little longer.*"? Or shame and its gangrene limbs, "*how could you let yourself be so viscerally seen?*"?

So when I grappled the branches of my body out of his embrace and made a beeline for the exit, I probably did run too fast. I probably didn't think. I'd done so much waiting that action felt exhilarating and my feet couldn't keep up.

I toppled up the stairs onto that crimson floor, and they say my head met the hard granite. I don't remember much of those exact moments except the sweat on my skin turning bitterly cold. I told you, I'm dramatic. And now here we all are, gathered today, under the golden ceiling, beneath an inadequate photograph, to bid a sweet, solemn goodbye to me. And the prince who was chasing me? They even invited him. I think I saw him crying earlier.

Watching it all unfold feels hallowed and silly. They're playing my life on a montage, but it doesn't look like the life I knew. Where is the dirt? Where is the ache? Where are the butterflies that kept me company and the beeswax candles I made from scratch? What is this insistence that we make the ending palatable? Show me crying, show me yelling, show me being battered from heartbreak. That is, *was*, my life. It is worth remembering it *all*, I think.

And so here I am, watching, still making the waiting something beautiful. Remembering, through the service, what it felt like to exist.

It probably is my fault. Glass slippers were always a bad idea.

DEAR SHE

KELLIE HANNAH

For Natalie, inspired by you and our shared journey, deepening our connection and waking up the ancestors. For Amy, patchouli twin, you are truth hope, love, joy, and friendship.

11:11 xx S, I'll meet you there
There was a glimmer, a moon, a star
There was the softness from afar
There was a feather, there was a song
There was a guidance all along
There was a bird who danced in flight
Free, so free just like that kite
There was a number on the ground
Eleven reminders could be found
There was so many soft things to see
There was a friend who is always free
I'll meet you there when it's your time
And up till then, look for the signs.

Some believe that when life ends, so do we. Others feel our presence stays, watching over and guiding from another place. I believe every moment in life matters, every experience is carried with us. When our time here ends, it has not been for nothing. We take with us the essence of our lives, and our energy stays, present and connected. One day, we will all know what comes after. For now, I offer you a different kind of guide – unlike my ancestors, known only through faded photographs, and some not even known. Imagine this as a page from a journal once kept by your great-great-grandmother, arriving in your hands just when you need it most. Her whispers passed down, her letter of learnings. I believe that just as programming and conditioning can be inherited, so too can the love and quiet knowing of those who came before.

In these words, you may see yourself, the one who gives more than she receives, the compassionate one, the strong one, the cup-filler, the fixer, the brave one. The one who is everything to everyone. In these words, you may find your own worth.

From above, she sees herself walking the sandy track, every step a conversation between her feet and earth, the smell of salt drifting into her every breath with its taste of peace and quiet. The distant drumming of the waves echoing a calling. Her calling. She knows it is time to listen. Shadows on the horizon, skeletons of the past reflecting back. Sunlight dancing across wild waves. Sitting crossed legged where the soft meets the hard, her favourite, her home, the sand breathing as the water retreats. A repetition, a spiral, the same and different every time. She knows to go in requires bravery.

Dear *She*,

Take a moment and sit, love. A moment to feel, to just breathe, you do not need permission to be, only an open heart. *She* sees you, even when it feels like you are not. *She* is the quiet knowing deep within your belly, an inner nudge, a tingling along your spine, the shiver over your shoulders. *She* is your intuition, your silent remembering, listen and you will hear.

There is a long line of strong women behind you, they carry you in their spirit, holding you when you need to be held, hearing what you most wish for. They were once like you, some loud, busy, some quiet, still, some celebrated, others silenced. Each having similar choices but not of the same circumstances in time. Strength is required in our world, our lineage and within the feminine. Not the kind worn boldly on your sleeve for all to see but an inner strength, one you go searching for, it is soul deep. On days when it cannot be found, *she* will be right there, within your intuition, within your synchronicity, within your heart.

There is a girl with a strong spirit and soft heart, she is the one who picked up from those before her, the programming, the repetition of the past and our stories. She had forgotten who she was, she had forgotten why she was here. She began to only exist. She is the daughter, the sister, the wife, the mother, the friend, the all – for everyone. She is determined, forgiving, puts everyone's needs above her own who in return takes nothing. A subconscious agreement, binding her to the story, a past story, an old story. Silenced as those before her were, living by a set of programs long instilled, from a space that felt safe, that had just become.

So, love, in case no one has told you, you can hold your truth, hold it tight, you are allowed to lead with your heart, feel it all. You can be the one who knows but not invests in it all. The one who says no, no more. The one that it stops with. You can evolve, be free from the past, take the lessons, and move on with these learnings. You are allowed my love, to do anything, this is your life, your story to write, to be seen as all of you. Make mistakes, live authentically, find your abundance, and remember your why.

There will be a day you will wake and begin to remove the armour you have worn for too long. An armour worn in by the feminine before. Imprinted with time and holding the stories from those before. It feels familiar, like your favourite jacket, the one that you never thought you would throw away because you have worn it for so long. When you are ready, you will recognise that it no longer fits, a hand-me-down, a subconscious contract and it will be then that you will know it is time for change. You will be terrified, feel naked, and you will seek your default, although this time, you won't. This time will be the first time you know that you are in control, you get to decide who you are, what you wear and how you wear it. It most likely won't be loud, the programmed guilt and fear will keep it quiet, there will be no shouting as though it requires a form of announcing, it will just be, it will just become, once you grant yourself the permission. Now this will not happen overnight, not in just one undressing, there will be many fittings, many adjustments, after all it is a tailor-made jacket for you to wear! It will take some time to wear it in, to cease operating from an unspoken expectation of self, an unspoken judgement, rejection, fear, silencing, this programming has been disguised as love. Not intentional by any means, blessed to be loved, it is just learnt, just repetitive. Just like a spiral, out and out and out she goes, the same but different, every time until it stops with you. Let it stop with you.

You are the one your great grandmothers prayed for, the one who knows it will be messy, but the one still prepared to go there. You speak the words they could not. You confront the silence ingrained. You are the one who remembers, and every time you do, you honour your lineage. You do not only exist, you live fully. Unpolished and most certainly with not everything figured out. You listen to your timing, your inner compass.

Magic, they say.
Well, I don't know about that.
There is nothing magic in timing.
That is intuition.
And you better listen to that.
Our compass, our guide, our very ride.
It is not magic you see.
It is just a way I try to be.

Now my love, there will be people in your life that will challenge, trigger, try to keep you in a space they know and not recognise the frequency you now hold. Not knowing the permission you have granted yourself. And you will default, you will dabble back and forth in that space that expectation, back and forth, round and round until you see yourself, until you feel it more than you think it, until you are seen, and then, dabble no more. For you are the author of every chapter, and you now trust that they will do the work when it is right for them, just as you will, just as you are. There is no right time, there is only your time. Your time to lean into every corner, every lesson, every mistake, every moment. What needs to find you will, it will come when you least expect.

You will recognise her, she is living in your timeline, maybe even your lineage. She is your mirror, a reflection, doing her own work, choosing the ripples she sends out, choosing her spiral, choosing her softening. Creating her own abundance, following her compass, and gifting you a compassion, a surrender, an understanding, a presence that feels like home. She will find you, you will find her, most likely when you least expect it, most likely when you most need it. A little synchronicity, a lot of similarity, a little timing, a lot of truth, sent to you, a little reminder like that shiver. She is in your story, and that is not a coincidence, it is a prayer from your past.

This is where you will softly begin. Quietly at first. It will ride from your womb, through your belly to your throat where you will express or suppress, evolve or repeat. When you are ready, you will know. When you are ready, those before will be present in your voice, their love in your story, their strength in your heart, their shivers across your shoulders and that knowing within your belly. You know it is in your softening, that you will be guided, in the compassion you now have for yourself that you will feel them. This is where your chapter starts, this is what has rippled through, this is their loudest whisper, their loudest reminder to you and they will hold you gently while it all shows up.

You will know when you have had enough.
It will show up in every moment, in every space.
The old walking itself out the door, the new waiting for its turn.
This is evolving.

And you will begin to gently hold the losses, the learnings. You have learnt it is in the gentle compassion for self, something gifted to others so easily and now bringing gifts to you. It will suffocate the need for blame or validation, this self-compassion will suffocate the need for any repeat. Knowing that love does not have conditions, and if it does, it is not love. So begin, start placing love with yourself, your own judgements, your own worth, your old story.

To begin again is no small feat.
Starting out in the driver's seat

Expect a rough and wild ride.
Expect an ever-moving tide.
This is not just one simple choice.
In every again, you will find your voice.

You see, something happens when you find your softness, when you speak to yourself the same way you speak to others. Eventually it becomes a habit, a conscious choice, and it feels like your grandmother's hand resting on your back, a little pat, warm and light. Cheering you on like you are the race winner, clapping loudly for all the times she was never clapped for, releasing the 'no's she held in her ripples, gifting you a connection, gifting you a guidance that's been there all along, it just needed softness to be felt.

Soften before roaring Leo
You are allowed to rest
It isn't in your toughness
That you will find your best
It's in the quiet softening
That you will feel the shift
It's in the quiet softening
That you will know the gift
She sent it to you late one night
Hoping you would hear
Her roar is always there you see
Right behind you, dear
She'll roar for you while you soften
Her hand around your heart
She'll show you how to listen
You just have to start.

So, sweet girl, know that when I pray these words, it will help shape your beginning of belonging to self. Once that is found, once it is seen, you will not go back, you will be operating from a different place and space. Stepping out from the repetition, out from all that you have been told. Finally, you will wear your worth, your why, just like that tailor-made jacket, designed exactly as you want it to be, in your favourite colour, with room for the adjustments you choose, ready for the story you write. And now, I leave you with my parting wish and deepest loving intention to find your compassion, find your worth, find your compass, and know you are guided, always. xx

From above, she sees herself walking the sandy track, her shoulders back, tall and solid like the old guardian trees around her, humming quietly, her feet feel the sand beneath, hearing the distant drumming of the waves, she feels no rush, no conditions. She will get there in time. Her time. Sitting crossed legged where the soft meets the hard, her favourite, her home. Sunlight dancing across wild waves. She presses the shell to her ear. She hears the softness in that hush. There it is. There are no hesitations, no bravery needed, she knows this time she is going in, right in, and with softness supporting her, she floats, she feels, she frees.

KELLIE HANNAH lives her life on the land, alongside her husband on their third-generation farming property in Western Queensland. Through writing, she's come to know a quieter kind of freedom. In this season of life, she allows herself to be fully seen, and to belong exactly as she is. Her work has been published online and in the *Anthologia* series.

@kelhannah.author

THE PETRICHOR PROJECT

S. JO-ANNE

On being human; our greatest gift and power.

Thud. Thud. Thud.

It was eerily overcast as a group of us, which made up the aid team, stepped cautiously onto the tarmac. This was during a period of time plagued by a string of disasters, war, floods, crises and the spread of disease around the globe. I wanted to make a difference where I could, so I had ventured with a team to a once-beautiful, vibrant island that was now washed over with a murky filter of brown. As we had neared the airport to land, I had conjured an image in my mind from the first time I had visited some years before. Yet now, as we drew closer to landing in the heart of the disaster zone, I could see everything had changed.

Forever.

As we collected our baggage and moved through the small airport, the task of the work ahead weighed on our minds. Each of us had been assigned a role. I was tasked with painting and providing general support for the students and orphans. I didn't have any trade skills to offer the team, but I had begged to come nonetheless. Between the group of us, we offered a complete skill set for site restoration. Although we had been informed of what we were walking into, our hearts still broke as we absorbed the reality of it all and met face to face with an island in peril.

Thud. Thud. Thud.

Being just nineteen at the time, my eyes had never been acquainted with the stark reality of what humanity looks like after a natural disaster. The picture of such devastation has been a driving force for me through my twenties and, as I write this now on the anniversary of this trip, I remember it all vividly. Children suffering with disease and injuries, elderly helplessly watching on as others sorted through piles of ruined household items, the ringing of crying on the street, the sound of axes and hammers clanging against metal as locals tried to piece *something* back together. Stains as high up on the walls as rooftops, where the water had violently risen, and a trail of debris where it receded.

I remember precisely where I was when the news broke because I frantically messaged my dear friends at the mission. I remember the feeling as though my heart had plummeted into my stomach. Over a million homes were reduced to mere rubble, leaving millions more displaced individuals. I cannot begin to imagine what it feels like to watch your home be swept away. Or your loved ones. How cruel it felt to know that every single person we passed as we left the airport had lost someone and something. No one was untouched by grief or loss. Not one soul.

Thud. Thud. Thud.

The drive to the mission was a quiet one. My eyes followed the rubble with each bend we wound along, my heart threatening to burst from my chest. I had fled something in Australia to be part of this trip. I had leapt at the opportunity to board a plane and throw myself into something more worthy of my time than self-wallowing and pity. My eyes were still puffy from the restless nights and crying.

He had cheated on me. I'd had an isolated, difficult time growing up. I often felt too creative and quirky to fit in. The relationship had been my first real one, and I thought we would get married. I had grappled with self-worth in the aftermath, left heartbroken. So, when the opportunity to join this team arose, I didn't hesitate to make arrangements. Call it divine timing, God's will or sheer coincidence; I took my chance to escape. Yet the heaviness of being recently heartbroken weighed on me like a damp cloak as we entered the disaster zone head-on.

As we drew nearer to the mission grounds, I was pulled into a grey space of polarity. Wedged firmly between my own grief and the grief of an island that had been devastated. The two felt incomparable. My pain was in no way comprehensively or remotely close to the magnitude of devastation I saw on the island. I could see *this* devastation with my own eyes. It looked like starving children and homes reduced to piles of ruin. It looked like bodies in bags and grieving parents. It looked like army trucks and aid teams digging through ruins to free animals from rubble and locate missing persons. No, the internal landscape of pain I had been lost within was no match for what my eyes saw. So I concluded on that drive that these two types of pain and loss were incomparable. I shoved mine down and focused.

Thud. Thud. Thud.

Mud and debris sprawled dust behind us as we pulled into the children's home and mission. I remembered how beautiful this sanctuary had been before. Branches were scattered by the entrance as we bounced across the potholes in the muddy driveway. We neared the main building, the dorms, a simple concrete flat roof structure, at the end of the driveway. Once painted white, now marred with debris and water stains. Three worn faces were waiting to greet us.

Frail but strong in spirit, there stood a bright little girl between them, waiting with such anticipation. With curly hair cascading over her petite shoulders, lively brown eyes watched intently as we all climbed out of the car. Despite the devastation that had enveloped us on the drive here, the sight of these three humans before us was a welcoming one. After we had gathered our luggage, we approached the steps where something tugged at me inwardly, in my own numbness, at the sight of a friend standing before me. Gratitude. I strained to hold back tears.

I let a small bubble of laughter escape as we all embraced in greeting. I noticed the little girl still wore the pendant around her neck that I had gifted her on my first trip. I tried to smile and sport a convincing brave face to hide the way I was crumbling internally. The greetings were fleeting though, because soon after, our aid team was guided through the property, assessing the home to measure the task before us.

The air hung thick with salt and sorrow as we trod softly along the pathways that weaved between buildings, the scent of the ocean mingling with dampness from crumbled walls and rotting, splintered wood. Just beyond the main centre of the site, we discovered the beach I had fallen in love with on my first trip was now polluted with heaps of litter, fragments of fishing nets, and displaced tree limbs stripped from their roots. The water had clawed its way inland, tearing away sandbanks and trees.

Students and caretakers alike worked across the property with blistered hands and raggedy clothes to clear the wreckage. It dawned on me that we came prepared with building and medical supplies, but I hadn't thought to pack any clothes to give away. While lined with exhaustion, their eyes always lit up when I caught a stray glance, and every single person we passed greeted us warmly.

By evening fall, we were acquainted with our rooms. The following morning, after a challenging time trying to sleep while fighting off mosquitoes, I rolled up my sleeves and joined the line in the main foyer. I realised, as we completed our morning brief and safety instructions, that this mission wasn't just about restoring the home. It was about *restoring hope too.* The children, the staff; they were all watching us. Fiercely. Intently. We were reminders of an outside world untouched by tragedy in this moment for them. Carriers of hope.

There is something to be said about the power of presence in times of turmoil. It is a gift to be a carrier of hope, but also a tremendous responsibility and privilege.

I did my best again to exude reassurance that everything would be OK. But honestly, that felt like a rich thing to do considering I was waging war internally with myself, stricken with grief and shame, loaded with questions about the heartbreak I had carried with me across oceans. Disbelief. Anger. The insatiable thirst for justice for my self. Still, I shoved it all down and focused on my job.

Thud. Thud. Thud.

It had taken a couple of months for us to construct the team and seek approval to travel to the area. The staff had already begun reconstructing what they could. Progress was slow initially, as they needed to focus on clearing the area before any real restoration could happen. Knowing that we weren't even seeing the worst of the situation on the island was heartbreaking all over again. I was now tasked with repainting the walls in the female section of the dorms. The scent of paint soon clung to everything. It curled in my nose, pressed into the back of my skull, leaving me with headaches for days to come. Still, I kept moving. A bandana became a necessity. Although the sweltering heat and humidity had me sweating profusely underneath it, I strapped that thing on every day diligently.

In the first few days of the trip, as I settled into a routine, I felt something solidify inside me. I really struggled with guilt, because it felt selfish to place any real value on what I was dealing with when the locals were in more physical and emotional pain than I was. They had lost more. Suffered *more.* The guilt I felt kept me up at night, so much so that I tossed and turned frequently. This emotional tug of war I was struggling with begged a question to surface; *is pain measurable?*

I had fled home and betrayal, desperate to drown the memories. Yet instead of escaping the pain, here it was. It had followed me, like my own shadow. Surrounding me, infiltrating my thoughts; I found myself ruminating as I set to work each day. By the end of the first week, I had built a prison in my mind. Walls that I began to shove all my shame, pity and confusion into, like a box. I tried to dismiss my heartbreak entirely. I tried to haul it in, lock it up and throw the key away because I felt silly and ashamed I had been heartbroken at all. *You have nothing to be sad about; look around you,* I would tell myself. And quietly, the little girl inside of me withered each time I did. The little version of me who longed to be seen and heard; she wept.

Thud. Thud. Thud.

The humidity wrapped around us like a heavy, wet blanket as we worked. Some days, it rained, and I could see the worry spread across faces of the children and caretakers as they warily looked out over the sea. It saddened me to see the fear, but I noticed something miraculous too. While some cursed the rain, some danced in it. Delighted in it. Some were gloriously undignified in the rain, and on one occasion, our team joined the children in hopping between puddles during an afternoon downpour.

Joy. It taught me how to find joy in the midst of rebuilding from ruin. I still wrestled with my emotions, but those moments were pure bliss and an important part of the journey this trip would take me on.

We paused work only to eat, meals mostly consisting of rice with chicken, and *always* a lovely plate of fruit. An older woman made every meal as beautiful as she could, and I admired the way she fed the entire home each day from a makeshift kitchen in a tent with the help of a few volunteers. It was in the second week, when I was bringing my empty plate to the wash bay, that she pulled me aside.

'How are you?' she asked quietly, cupping my head between her frail hands.

The gesture took me by surprise.

'How are you?' she repeated.

I swallowed, looking away for a second.

'I will be fine.'

She clicked her tongue and released my face, turning toward the small washbasin.

'You, fight, you,' she offered over her shoulder as she began tossing dirty dishes about in the basin.

I stared at her hands, chewing my lip. Her broken English said plenty with so few words.

You. Fight. You.

I thought my first serious relationship would undo me gently, receding the same way it came. Instead, it had broken me like the sea breaks the spine of a coastal tree.

Yes, I am fighting myself.

~

The sun hadn't yet crested fully over the hills when our team was led to the edge of a small clearing past the student classrooms some days later. It wasn't a field yet, just a patch of sodden earth, still muddy in places from the flood that had waterlogged the property. The old vegetable patch, they informed us, was gone. I was handed a hoe and shown how to turn the soil. The clearing was not very large, but was enough to replant some necessary vegetation for the home. The field was hemmed in by fallen trunks and splintered ribs of coconut palm trees, but as the students helped to carry baskets of debris away, the clearing took shape.

The older woman soon arrived with a tray of water bottles for us. She set it down and stood quietly at the edge of the turned, soft dirt, watching as I methodically ploughed into the soil and turned it over. When I went to get some water after finishing my row, she smiled and pointed to the dirt.

'You,' she says, pointing at me, 'put heart in dirt.'

She motioned to her chest where her heart is, then to the field where I had turned the dirt over.

Confused, I looked at her for a moment before I realised she was talking about my emotions. Well, she must have been. I nodded, and a smile found its way to my face as I reached forward and squeezed her shoulder.

'I will plant new seeds then.'

~

I realised over the course of the next two weeks that we weren't painting over the damage to conceal it or patching up damaged goods. We were making this space liveable again, *beautiful* again, erecting a new home from the remnants of an old one that had served its purpose until it simply could not withstand the floodwaters.

What a privilege it is to build something new. I kept the promise I had made that day on the field. I decided to try to plant some new seeds, to find forgiveness while I detoxified my mind by busying my hands with the task before me each day.

Whatever is in front of me today, just do that *excellently,* I would affirm each morning before leaving my dorm room. If it was helping repair doors and windows, tending to the newly ploughed vegetation patch, or removing debris from the beach, I did my best to do it all excellently. Purposefully.

And as the trip neared an end, I found the grip that guilt had over me in the beginning began to loosen. I had shed many tears, for myself and for those around me. But as a team and a healing village, we had also laughed together. Grown together. As time passed, the kind of wisdom that is only found in hindsight began to whisper to me that all would be well in my world again. I learned, and have been reminded time and time again since, that healing is much like rebuilding an orphanage.

Healing is never linear and often very nuanced, requiring no shortage of courage and grit. Healing isn't about erasure. It isn't about pretending the cracks aren't there or trying to escape the storm; many things are out of our control. True healing starts with *standing in the ruin and picking up the hoe to do the work*, because the only way to alchemise loss or pain is to keep building. Just like my brave friends did.

The question I asked myself is married with an answer then: *can pain be measured?* Could I measure or stack up my grief over heartbreak against the pain the locals felt in the wake of a devastating natural disaster? No, these two types of pain are immeasurable and incomparable, but they are equally valid, and both must be given shape. Both must be alchemised through the act of setting out to create a new home, or relationship, or job, or perception of self. Pain, by nature, is disruptive. It dismantles the version of a reality we once knew, leaving behind fragments of what was. Pain can feel paralysing. But just like physical pain requires healing, emotional pain doesn't transform by itself either. Pain only transforms when we sit and engage with it, when we give it shape, meaning and set it alight with motion. Building is that motion. It is the act of saying, 'I will not let this be the end of the story.'

On the evening before we were due to fly back, I watched the sunset and vowed to rebuild myself, to repaint the walls inside of me and make a safe sanctuary out of a space that had been tumultuous for months leading into that trip. The thudding of my chest had subsided. The feeling of guilt and shame was replaced with purpose. I wrote those vows in my phone, a final task of purging and resolve to conceal the trip. I read them aloud to the night sky as it opened up before me, moonlight poking through gaps of cloud cover which soon began to release droplets. When I boarded the plane the following day, I counted my blessings instead of sorrows; and my heart was full.

~

This humanitarian mission changed me in profound ways. First, a constant reminder to find perspective and make vows that still guide me. Second, something was born in me, a tangible pull toward my life's work. The latter years of our teen lives are deterministic. We begin to weigh up our relationship with free will and decide what kind of people we will be in this world. At just nineteen, I had a choice: to shut down or lean in. I chose to lean into the pain, to embrace the experience and let it crack me open.

I'm a grown woman now with unwavering conviction about what I want to create with the time I have on this earth. I have made many choices and mistakes alike in my twenties. I have won some and failed equally. These lessons have guided me through navigating an ambitious career as a business and marketing strategist, whether in high-stakes boardrooms or complex negotiations. I've built brands, teams and strategies in spaces where I wasn't always welcomed or valued, and I've grappled with misogyny, harassment, and loss many times along the way. The world can be loud and unfair sometimes, but as women, if we quiet ourselves to let purpose, not fear, shape our paths and decisions, we step into our power. I have grappled with how to tell this story for the past decade, but one word kept coming to me. I stumbled across '*petrichor*' some years ago and the meaning of it deeply resonated*: the smell produced when rain falls on dry ground, usually experienced as being pleasant.*

I felt compelled to frame this chapter as a call to action rather than just a retelling of an important season in my life. I hope you see The Petrichor Project as a commission, whether you're a career woman, a mother, a friend, a wife, a dreamer; a commission to leave this place better than when you found it. To savour the scent after the rain. Remember, some cursed the rain. Some danced in it.

Who will you be?

If you're standing in the ashes of loss or grief and you're looking for something to take away from this story, it's OK to start right where you are; in the ashes. Just as I did all those years ago. Build something honest from that place. Build. Because that's how pain becomes power. In retelling the stories that have shaped us the most as women, as humans, we retrieve the parts of ourselves lost to life, circumstance or people; and we reclaim them. Perhaps the most incredible thing that happens when we commit to healing is that we create new pathways not just for ourselves, but for others too. We need the writers, the artists, the policymakers, the scholars, the technologists, the healers and the stoics to stay committed to making beautiful things again from ordinary, difficult and challenging circumstances. Because in the quiet when the world is stripped down to splinters and silence, what's left is not ideology, not borders, not politics; but people. I believe humanity shows its truest face not in comfort, but in action.

I saw people share their last handful of rice with strangers on that mission. I saw survival braided with compassion. There were no language barriers, religious disparities or separations of ideologies in the ruins. Just human beings, holding each other up. True power comes when we learn to reckon with the parts of ourselves we aren't proud of, the parts of ourselves that have bled and hurt; and choose to rebuild something of substance.

The version of you that entered the chasm is not the same version that emerges. And that is a wonderful, potent gift. Hold on to it.

In crisis, our humanity is the most valuable resource we have.

When everything else is gone, being human is all we have left. And it is not a weakness; it is our power.

With a background in journalism and marketing, **S. JO-ANNE**'s work has been featured in leading Australian newspapers and various outlets, focusing on stories that inspire resilience and transformation. Now through the Shekinah House Organisation, S. Jo-Anne is focusing on creating a mission-driven platform that amplifies stories, empowers women, and supports meaningful change. With a deep commitment to building community around purpose-driven social impact work, S. Jo-Anne's mission is to uplift, empower, and inspire; one story, one project, and one connection at a time.

shekinahhouse.org

THE BOY

JOANNE WILLMOTT

For Jack —
for every atom belonging to me as good belongs to you.

To my darling son, my darling boy. I've been trying to write this letter for so very long. Years. You know how I put things off until the very end. But now, I feel them getting closer, I need to get this down, quickly. Time is slipping. Time. I'm writing with my favourite pen, the one with the timber finish and the gold top. Well, it's nearly out of ink. I'm annoyed at myself. I should've refilled it. I meant to. I put it somewhere safe. The cartridge. I think. Maybe in a pocket. I need you to know. In case something happens. In case they come.

Before you were born. 2001. The eleventh of September. It was a usual night for me. Alone in the house. Waiting for you. I couldn't sleep, moving from one side and over to the next. I decided to get up. Lying in bed was useless. Staring at the beautiful moulding along the ceiling, even in the dark, I could make out all the glorious rivets and twirls. I could no longer lie there, chewing the fleshy corner of my mouth. I stood up as best I could, pushing the bed away to stand. My belly so wonderfully full of you. Six glorious months. Six marvellous months pregnant with you.

The bedroom was opposite the lounge room, so not much of a walk. I'm not sure if you remember the fireplace. The fireplace in our first home. Oh, how I imagined families before us. Maybe a father, a shipyard worker, telling tales. The room a stage, and he lit from behind with the embers cracking. A quiet mother sitting stoically. Children on their tummies, with their chins resting in their pretty palms, right on the edge of their imagination.

I'd left the television on, you know, for company and to trick intruders. You know how I do that now. A pair of large shoes outside. Men's. You can never be too careful. Breaking news. To my horror, the Twin Towers in New York were exploding. The Twin Towers. It was 10.05 pm exactly. It said so on the television. We were a million miles away, but I'm certain you felt the tremor. I'm sure you did. Those big feet of yours stomped against my belly. The second plane, like a drunk driver, dip, dip, turn. People on the street tilting up to see their world change forever. Tall clouds of debris. Children who would be without their mothers or fathers that night. Oh, the horror. Hats, shoes, the soot thick, people walking out of the dust. Handprints on café windows, with fingers' prints searching for the door. Journalists charging across the streets like troops to cover the scene.

Prime Minister Howard would say in time, on *Sixty Minutes*, 'That as awful as it sounds, as a calculation designed to humiliate, it could've been better.'

I'm trying to explain how that night changed everything. I will tell you. This pen. This damn pen. Where did I put the cartridge? And it keeps slipping from my hand.

Your first home – a white, weathered workman's cottage tucked along a long suburban road, just before it collided with the busy main street – we were right next to the local store. It had a corrugated metal roof, with two street-front windows. Sturdy plantation shutters. A charming front veranda with a white picket fence. Our garden out front: wildflowers, the crimson padded kangaroo paws, a plethora of busy ferns that were neatly chopped at the top. At the far end of the street, the dark brown brick housing estates began, with magnificent views over the Parramatta River.

I could hear our house, it was always speaking to me – softly, tiptoes paced – I could follow the sounds running breathless. I'm sure I could hear them. I certainly saw its shapes most days. Silhouettes out of the corner of my eye, scampering from the room as I entered.

The bedroom was small, in keeping with the house. But oh, how lovely. I had to push the queen bed right up to the window to make space. Your cot, still empty, waited for you. Lemon sheets edged with duck-egg blue. Oh, how many hours I spent pacing up and down the main street, possessed by indecision. Possessed, I tell you. They had to be just perfect. No washed-out colour. No random threads. I furiously shopped, as if late for an appointment. An appointment that didn't exist.

The room faced the road. Out front, morning magpies with their pretty white clerical collars fluffed as they would row over bread, or a tin of emptied fish. The clanking they would make. Oh, the carry-on. Then those damn developers, always on the street, swooping down and cutting corners, their claws stretching to the riverside estates. Single-floor homes were marooned amongst the newly constructed high-rises. They would stand on the street right outside our window, squawking about the trophy location.

There was a constant rumble beneath, a clickety-clack. The slow shuffle of grassroots folk picking up their swag to move on.

Most mornings, in the house, before you were born, I would prop myself up with pillows, hands resting greedily on my belly.

'This is your new home,' I'd whisper, tracing slow, circular patterns across my t-shirt, worn thin, spills of tea or juice from watermelon. The waiting. The smallness of the world reduced to that room, that corner. You were not here yet, but my beautiful boy, how you already filled the space.

This damn pen. I'm forever shaking it, but if I don't get this down before I go, I'm not sure I ever will. You know how forgetful I can be.

Did I tell you I went to boarding school? This. Damn. Pen. Of course I did. I need to tell you though. I know I speak suddenly, and flit from topic to topic. But they are coming, and I must tell you. And I'm running out of time.

Eleven years old. The world awkward and enormous. Almost as enormous as the Victorian stairs I had to climb all alone. Clunk, clunk, clunk went my bag, my little arms aching. I turned back for one last look. I had already kissed my parents goodbye, with a little smile, my little heart pounding.

I must tell you this.

Inside the dorm, greeted by a line of stern timber cupboards. Sparse hangers. A row of beds, each with an awful uniformed grey army blanket. Iron bars on the windows. My stomach fell. Fell right down under the earth. I didn't think a stomach could fall so far, I ran, hurried, to the top of the stairs.

'Don't leave me here.'

But they were already gone.

And something, whatever it was that made me a child, went with them.

I whisper as I write, my darling, these secrets I must tell. But I want you to understand, I tried to keep you safe. The best way I could.

You arrived. In November. First of the season. A perfect little apricot, plump and golden.

I must skip a bit for the sake of time. I don't mean to edit out your birth. No, not at all. Please forgive me. I must get this down. Oh, you were beautiful. That is all you need to know. More beautiful than a heaven of angels. I saw all their faces in you. There is not a word that could ever describe you. For now, an apricot will do. Sweet, sweet boy. I know that if there is a good God, he surely made you.

We're not home today. We're making daisy chains on a hibiscus sarong. Your long toes, and long legs. Your golden hair, and caramel eyes. So elegant. Not like me. Not like me at all. I will leave the tap running. The fridge door open. Towels on the line for days.

In the evenings, when you are wrapped perfectly in muslin, I would swaddle your first arm, then swaddle your legs. Our faces mirrored with laughter as I popped you into your cot, standing until your lips made gentle puckers, and I knew you were asleep. Most evenings, I would smoke out the back, looking out to the yard while you slept. I would grieve – because my milk never came in. That's why I took up smoking again. When I swore I would not. Grief makes us do the strangest things.

Pump, pump, pump.

My breasts held back tears. It wasn't safe to express.

I would sit at the backyard door, cold timber beneath, the cool evening shivering, and gaze at the cracked concrete I lifted while pregnant, my bare hands planting rosemary and thyme. I could smell the soil rising in the evenings, damp, as the lovely Korean couple who owned the store next door argued. And wish for someone to protest to. Just to hear my own voice outside of my head. Not the incessant throbbing at my temples. Not just speeches in my skull till the bones would splinter.

Then the nights you went limp in my arms, eyes rolled back – the ambulance came. I ran out barefoot, you in my arms as if offering you to the gods.

'Febrile convulsions, he'll be alright. Put some clothes on, Miss, before ya jump in.'

I stood impotent in my underpants and t-shirt.

There will be more. The routine. The paralysis before dialling.

Triple-zero. Breathe.

Some days, we'll sit on the front step. Days when I'm feeling brave. When the sun is not too bright, and the developers are scarce.

'It's lovely seeing you outside with your baby. You don't see that anymore ...'

The lovely barrister and his wife, the accountant, who live two houses down. Eventually, we'll have dinners together. The three of us carrying you back in after, trying not to wake you, giggling with red wine smiles.

Then the visitors will come with their gifts wrapped in judgement and concerns. I probably shouldn't say that, but I knew they didn't care for my company. I would spend days in the lead-up madly cleaning and scrubbing. Ironing tablecloths. Washing teacups until they squeaked. Buying flowers. A bunch for every room. With different perfumes. Hosing down the veranda just before they came, with a finishing splash of eucalyptus oil. All while you watched. Alone. You felt my panic. I'm sure.

I would dress you in a beautiful blue outfit. You had a few I would rotate so there was always something clean and at the ready. One pretty dress. For me.

They will come. On various days and suitability. To them.

They would coo. Why wouldn't they? You were so perfect, and I so proud of you. Such a cheeky thing, as all babies should be.

I will hope they comment on the clean house, the dress, the flowers, and the slices plated for them.

'You're looking thin.'

'Your eyes are dark.'

'Have you been smoking?'

I will move into the background to make room for them. Fingertips red raw. In my pockets. No one will mention the dress.

Damn bloody pen. The ink is starting to fade.

They would leave, and we would hear their hushed gossip float down the street. There was always a stench. I thought there might be a rat in the wall. I would check. The house would fall silent. And you would wonder where everyone went. You sat in your highchair as I cleaned up their plates and their cups, throwing their half-eaten things into the bin.

You shouldn't have had to watch. We should have been able to rest together. This damn pen.

Intrusive thoughts crept as my tired eyes would trace back to the moulding with its twists and turns. I would leave the tea in the microwave, beeping. You would giggle. Your cherub cheeks turned pink towards the ceiling. I would laugh with you. Press my nose against yours. Tickle you.

You knew. I knew you knew. The days punctuated with my stillness. Frozen. My face unreadable.

And the days you cried, because I was yelling. Your confused, frightened eyes searching. The storm had arrived. The hurricane. There was no one to shelter us. No one to shelter you. The world's voices huge black waves in my mind. Wild, invisible arguments that petrified you.

Do you want us to raise him?

You're the one who got yourself pregnant.

You're nuts. You're crazy.

I will respond to them, into the dark, how much I love you. If they would only stop torturing me. I will gnash and snarl into the night. I will undo, not like a kitten with a ball of string, but like a caged animal. Thrashing.

I'm trying to silence it. To keep it quiet. Shhh.

I'll sweep you into my arms, both of us crying hot, hot tears. I will kiss you a million sorries. The shame. Your beautiful face looking into mine, the face of your protector, yelling. Not understanding why. And me, not understanding why.

The next day, I would always make it better. Always. Ice cream. Cartoons. Finger painting. Cuddles all day. A lemon sheet over chairs and make-believe in our cubby place. Where no one could get to us. Where we were safe from them all to just be mother and child.

We visit the shop in the late afternoon. Jin and Kyung-soo will stroke your cheeks, cooing over how milk-white you are. I would hold you on my left hip, right hand on the pram, pour you like a porcelain teapot to breathe in the day's flowers.

They'll let you choose the bunch. Wrap them in bright paper. How you threw your head back and laughed. The centre of attention. Jin would slip chocolates into the pram. I would pretend not to notice. She'd be delighted, thinking of you finding them there.

The night came. We would settle. I draw you in, warm little chest pressed to mine. You're not in the cot on those nights. You needed me close. Calm. You would turn into me, green singlet soft against my skin, eyelids fluttering. Your breath steady. I would match it. Press my nose to your freshly washed hair. You smell sweet. Candy floss. Your small ribs rising. Falling. Our rhythm. Returned.

I imagined the mothers of this house watching, from the walls, rearranging the day's remorse into hushed song. Puffing pillows to rest our heads on.

The Enid Blyton book I read to you, *The Magic Faraway Tree*, rests in my hand, corners curled.

Some nights I want to run. This pen. I wish I could remember where I put the cartridge. I left it somewhere. Hand on the front door. I want to run away with you. But there's nowhere to go. No one waiting. I dream the most awful dreams. They had locked the door behind us. Locked us in. Forgotten. They got what they needed. My fingerprints scorched against the brass handle.

I have just enough time now. Just enough, I'm hoping. Just enough to tell you. Aha, the cartridge. Maybe it's in my back pockets.

I found my way back. Back to the house. As I write against the wall. The television is on. There are children crying. Different children on the television. Hungry. I can hardly look. With a different prime minister talking. I can't bear it. Can't bear it at all. You are all grown. The house, our house, had others in there. Can you imagine? But I pushed them all out. I chased them away. All the way down to the end of the street. I told them to go. I have let all the garden in. The ferns and the kangaroo paws. Kookaburras too. An eternal bookshelf reaches way up to the sky. Oh, it is wonderful. Just the way I wanted it. Before they all came. With their ways. The young soldiers have come alive from their posts outside, and I've sent them all home to their mothers.

I am exhausted. So very tired. My wrist heavy. I had to tell you this.

They stole from me. Oh, how they stole.

But they robbed you.

So, I've put it all back. Put it all back before I …

JOANNE WILLMOTT is a writer, journalist, speaker, and yoga teacher. She has lived with Bipolar Disorder, chronic pain, and nine psychiatric hospitalisations while raising her son on her own. She explores through her work how stigma directed at parents living with mental illness becomes the burden of the most vulnerable – their children.

@inclusivewellnessbyjo

SUMMERTIME SON

JACQUELINE GAUL

For Jack.

It's a cold winter's day and I'm watching your siblings play outside, climbing the old gum tree, gasping with laughter. But you – you are not here. Grey clouds stretch across most of the sky, with only fleeting glimpses of blue giving just enough to suggest the sun might return. The trees sway in the chill. Every so often, I catch the scent of incense drifting from the room next door – sandalwood, patchouli, vanilla – and for a moment, I could almost believe I'm in an exotic writers' retreat in Bali, not in this small office at the back of the house, next to the laundry, listening to the endless spin cycle in the middle of suburbia.

You weren't born in the cold. It was summer – one of those blazing Queensland summers where the sun shone relentlessly, and the humidity turned everyone's hair to frizz. We spent so much time in the ocean together, you and I. While pregnant with you, I loved being in the water. There's something magical about feeling weightless in saltwater, especially when carrying life. The ocean has always been my sanctuary, the place I turn to when life gets too loud. And somehow, I've always felt that you and I are connected through the sea.

You came into the world like a ripple, a gentle wave of love washing over me. I'd hoped for a water birth, though the hospital wasn't able to accommodate it. When my waters released, I felt an immediate warmth and comfort. Laying there in the liquid that once surrounded you was all-encompassing. We were so close in that moment, and yet I could feel the changing of the tide – the beginning of the goodbye. It was as if the sea itself came to collect you and carry you away. It was love and heartbreak all at once. And soon after, you were born.

You were so small, so perfect. You looked like you were sleeping, like you could stir at any second, take a breath and open your eyes to meet mine. But that moment never came. You left before I was ready to let you go. And although my arms were empty, the water never let you drift too far. Every time I am near the ocean, or immersed in a warm bath, I feel you. My little Pisces. My summertime son. Now, so far from any moving body of water, I feel that longing for you, for the ocean. I miss you, Jack, immensely.

It's been nearly four years since we moved to the Australian outback, and eleven years since I lost you. The contrast from the coast is sharp. There's no moisture in the air. For the first few weeks, our noses bled from the dryness. The water here is strange – we're on bore water, which leaves a slimy film on the skin and sometimes smells faintly of hard-boiled eggs.

The summers are brutal. Over forty degrees, with zero humidity. Stepping outside feels like entering an oven. Stay out too long and you'll come back inside looking like a marshmallow held too long over a fire.

Life out here is different in every way. Slower. Quieter. More isolating. At times, it has pushed me to my edge – and in that space, I've been forced to go inward. That has felt like both a gift and a burden. When you finally have time on your hands, you also meet the darker – and brighter – parts of yourself. I wrote a book while we've been here. 40,000 words poured out of my soul, and I shared this book with the world. I learned to stand up, to speak to a crowd, to be a leader. I met new people who filled me with knowledge and heart. I learned to be alone, I learned to live with grief – and I learned that grief never leaves you, just changes form with time. I've discovered a deep need for creativity: an outlet for the wounded and unhealed parts of me to be seen and transformed into something beautiful. Gifts to share with the world.

I doubt I would have done any of these things, had we stayed on the coast… or if you hadn't left the way you did.

That's the thing about change, it scares the living shit out of me when it is happening, but with a bit of time and space, I can look back and be grateful for what it gave me. Opportunities. New friendships. A version of myself I might never have met had everything stayed the same.

You were – and still are – the greatest catalyst for change in my life. Losing you was never something I imagined. It wasn't even a thought I entertained. I don't think many first-time mothers consider stillbirth a possibility. We go in believing we'll come home with a baby. And then sometimes, we don't. I went from feeling your kicks, preparing your nursery, to grieving your life – and the future that would never unfold. But with each passing year, I've come to realise: birthing you also birthed a different version of me.

Your father and I separated a few years after you were born. It wasn't because of you. The cracks were there before – but your birth, and your death, tugged hard on the frayed tapestry of our marriage, and eventually, what once resembled the image of a happy family slowly came undone.

For a long time, I carried guilt. I worried he wouldn't have more children – he was seven years older, and though still young, I feared it might be too late for him. A part of me felt responsible. It took years to forgive myself. And if I'm honest, I still carry that heaviness – the ripple effect of your brief life. So many hearts were touched by your coming and going. I wish I knew what to do to lighten the load – if that comes with time, or if that feeling will stay with me until the day we are reunited.

I did go on to have more children – two beautiful daughters. Your sisters. Time gave me the gift of second chances, of motherhood. I took the opportunity with both hands. I've been fortunate to be home with your siblings in their younger years and to watch them grow into the independent little women they are becoming. To be there for every kindy pickup and drop off, every performance, sports event and special moment. I've lived through the ache of missing those moments with you, and am learning to cherish the ones I get to have with them.

In our living room, we keep an altar for you. There's a wooden plaque with your name, a verse about you, and a small green butterfly carved from agate resting on a glass coaster etched with angel wings. The girls are drawn to it often. When they play, they hover near the altar, and as recently as two days ago, one of them added seven small rocks she painted at kindergarten to the space – many of them dotted with bright colours and decorated with love hearts.

My eldest daughter asks about you often. She asks me what happened, and why you aren't here. It feels impossible to answer her at times, because the truth is I still ask myself those same questions. *Why aren't you here? Why did your life end? Where did you go? Will we meet again?* I wish I could sit with you and ask you these questions and wonder if you'd be able to give me the answers I so desperately seek.

I wonder what you'd be like now, as an eleven-year-old boy. Would you be curious? Quiet? Mischievous? Your father was the keenest fisherman I've ever met. When he wasn't working as a tradesman, he was out on the water wetting a line. We spent many beautiful moments together on the water – fishing and cruising around. Would you have your father's love for fishing? Would you come home smelling of salt and seaweed? I imagine you knee deep in the mud collecting crab pots and working out when the tide is turning. Planning your next fishing trip and returning home to tell us the stories of the illusive one that got away.

One of the most beautiful sounds in the world is your name spoken aloud. Whenever I hear it – from a stranger, in passing – I stand a little taller. My ears sharpen. My heart tilts toward it. Is it you, I wonder? Is this a message? Or is it just hope, lingering?

Lately, I've been listening to an audiobook called *Signs* – stories of people connecting with loved ones who've passed in the most unexpected and magical ways. I've gasped, cried, felt my skin ripple with goosebumps. And above all, it has given me something I didn't realise I'd lost.

Hope.

Hope that although we are no longer together here on Earth, there is an invisible string that binds us: and maybe, just maybe, you can hear me when I speak to you.

With all my love,
Mum

JACQUELINE GAUL is a storyteller who through deep empathy, authenticity and personal experience, helps people heal and transform by embracing their own stories. She believes that our stories, no matter how messy, painful, or complicated, deserve to be told. Because when we share the truth of our lives, we connect, we heal, and we transform.

@jacquelinebgaul

SOFT ASH BRIGHT FLAME

ZOE PERRY

The greatest gift you can receive is to lose it all.
In that, you are nothing, and you are everything.

The call came that morning, and I just knew. The skies cried in sympathy as I swung into the carpark near the hospital entry and rushed through pelting rain. I entered the ward head down, lest someone witness the fear in my eyes and I shatter under their gaze. I held my breath as I entered Dad's room. He was flopped over on an angle, unable to stabilise himself – paralysed fully on the right side of his body. His eyes were out of focus, flickering side to side. Saliva ran from the corner of his mouth. He couldn't speak any words. Small groans came out of him as he tried to communicate, trapped inside his body that was no longer in sync with his brain. The sight of him in this state was unbearable. Terrifying.

Oh … Dad!

I slid off my Birkenstocks and climbed into his hospital bed to hold him in my arms. This was one of those times when you could feel the Earth rotating. Where you could conceive of your minuteness in the vastness of existence. Every sense dilated and sensitive to the stimulus around you. When nothing and everything mattered. At once I regressed to a state of child-like desperation but at the same time I began to stroke his face with a maternal reassurance. *I'm here, it's OK. I'm right here. I won't leave you.* I held his head against mine as my tears fell in a torrent. All I could hear over and over in my head was the thrum of the end – *this is it … this is it … this is it …*

He was gone in a matter of days. He took his last breath in my arms in the hospital bed. Dosed up on morphine and midazolam, weaving in and out of consciousness as I emptied myself of every word I'd ever wanted to say to him. *He can hear it all*, the nurses reassured me, *hearing is the last sense to go.* I kept on talking to him, hours after he was dead. Holding his hand until it was stiff and cold and the nurses needed to prepare the body for the morgue.

~

I woke to a salty breeze swaying the palms along my driveway, on a mild autumn morning in my home on the east coast of Australia. The kookaburras and lorikeets a blur of rainbow visions and laughter in the gumtrees outside my window. I stepped barefoot into the garden to feel damp lawn between my toes. The ocean glinted phthalo blue on the horizon as I stood sipping Robert Timms black coffee from an echidna mug gifted from Dad. I stared into the auburn rays, inhaling the aroma of geranium foliage at first light. What was there not to be grateful for: and yet, my lungs were clamped in a vice.

In the days and weeks after Dad's death, I lost myself in paint and pages. Tucked away in my home studio, I'd write and paint the pain out of my body. Gazing into the blur of colours and letters through tears that fell in rage and sorrow, I edged myself ever closer to truth, to beauty, to meaning in this profanity of existence. My dear heart; red rose petals through a meat mincer. I was only thirty-three; that felt too soon to lose my father.

I took myself inside and stared at my screen as golden light filtered through sheer curtains. With fingers lingering over keys, the words began to stream as my subconscious unravelled:

It's been 93 days since you died. A deep dark well of inky-black grief. Pulling me down into the overriding fullness of it. Memories playing out like visions as the tears loosen their grip on my cheeks and flow like a sorrowful dance across the structure of my face. I had to make the world stop yesterday, to catch my breath. To take some rest from the spinning when I needed to sink, to hold every memory of you in my fingertips and lay them gently down. I replay the end again and again hoping it will land. In a world where you used to live, and where I still feel you, but can't see you anymore. I'm heavy with the thought of you. With the death of you. With the lack of you. Three months and some days I feel like my legs are made of lead and I can't move at all. Three months and I feel I can't reach out and touch your memory so easily. I want to lay back down and go to sleep, maybe dream of you. I hope you know I love you and I think of you every day.

~

The leadup to Dad's death felt like a fast march through hell. In October we sat in the oncologist's office and learned the cancer was back. The terminal diagnosis surged through our lives like a tidal wave. *Adenocarcinoma.* Stage four, with no treatment options. By December he was gone. Eight weeks. The end came before we could even process that it was coming. He gradually grew weaker, slept more, ate less. The crushing pain of chronic headaches slowly grinded him down. The cancer weaved its parasitic damage through his lungs at such a rate that soon he couldn't sleep horizontal. He spent long nights coughing up blood and phlegm, trying to sleep upright on the couch. The coughing fits became so severe he'd gag and gasp for air, chest heaving with the effort. Breathless. Sleep deprived. Suffocating.

In the last weeks he bled from three separate orifices: a side effect of the high doses of blood thinning medication. He'd wake in the night to nosebleeds and a metallic taste on his palette. Hearing him spit mouthfuls of blood and saliva in the sink, I'd rush in to place gauze and pressure on his bleeding gums. I could smell the stench of death on his breath with my face so close to his. There was never any peace for him as I continued to advocate; driving him to appointments, asking questions of professionals, trying to keep him alive. I went into a kind of disassociation throughout this time. I wanted it all to be over – but I *never* wanted it to be over. Because then he would be gone.

There were days I felt like a caged animal as I navigated being a carer of the dying. I yearned for the past when things felt normal and my life felt like my own. Those precious days when I'd come to visit and we'd go out for coffee, wander the markets, have a meal at a nice restaurant and laugh as we pretended to be food critics. Now we were attending doctors appointments, MRI's, ultrasounds, PET scans, CT scans, oncology and neurology appointments. It was relentless. *Are you hungry, are you in pain, do you need pain killers, have you had your medication, do you need a rest, would you like to go outside, you look tired, have you had enough water …* I was always switched on in caring mode. But when my aunt or brother would come to give me respite, I could barely stand the panic of being away from him.

I cried often and at random times. Looking at carrots in the grocery store, laying on the reformer at the end of a pilates class, standing in line at a café for a coffee, walking down the street, during an online work meeting. It wasn't just the impending loss of my father that caused my emotional neurosis. It was the guilt, the regret, the questioning and critical self-evaluation of myself as his carer for the final months of his life. There were times I quietly lost my patience with his slowness or his pain, or his neediness of me. Then almost instantaneously I'd spiral into knots of self-loathing guilt and shame. *He's dying. What's wrong with me? I love him and he needs me. Why can't I be selfless?*

I'd taken on the idea that it was my sole responsibility to keep him alive.

~

Four months after his death, I realised I needed a circuit breaker to snap from my squandering self-pity. I boarded a plane and flew 10,000 kilometres across the Indian Ocean, my backpack filled with linen, watercolour paints and my sketchbook. I hoped to make peace with this grief in my bones. I'd heard of India as a place filled with temples, ashrams, holy rivers and ceremonies, and I went searching for the sacred that might show me the answers.

Landing on foreign earth, I lost myself in the throngs of 1.46 billion people. One white woman in a sea of honey faces. After a night to recalibrate in my hotel, I ventured into the streets of Delhi and found my way to a temple. Surely I would discover a god, an answer, some meaning here. I witnessed in reverie the vibrant scene around me. Intricately decorated silver trays spiralled round and round, aflame with burning offerings over the heads of temple dwellers. Hands clapping, voices chanting, incense burning and swirling. Eyes ablaze with the colour of marigolds offered in prayer to the gods. Cascading rose petals landed in my hair as I clapped to the beat of the ancient songs thrumming in my ears. The people made their way through the temple like ants scattering in the rain. They pushed, stared, smiled, and nodded as I chanted Sanskrit words that felt foreign in my mouth. Tears drifted downward, but not in relief; rather in the knowing that this sacredness was not mine. I could only be a witness to this devotion and glory. As I moved through the crowd I could find no clear channel to the divine in the distortion of chaos around me. The ritual and raucousness only acted as a distraction.

~

Healing and redemption can come from the places we least expect it, and I didn't find enlightenment in the Hindu shrines and temples. But pleasure can be a balm infused with frankincense and myrrh to those who find themselves crawling through the trenches of pain. As my pilgrimage to find peace from my grief progressed with my travels, the lure of a lover presented itself in the hot desert sands of Rajasthan.

After a six-hour journey south-west of Delhi, we edged towards the border of Pakistan. I stepped from air-conditioned vehicle into stifling arid air, and in 43-degree heat stood at the gateway of a sandstone castle. Black lichen sprawled across its fortress walls and spires. My eyes moved across the scene and fell upon a man walking away from the reception desk, fixated on his phone. The khaki fabric of his clothing clung to a tall, muscular frame. Emerald and gold studs shimmered on the honey-coloured lobes of his ears. And then – he looked up and my eyes met his: irises so dark they had the magnetic pull of black holes. Neither of us looked away as my feet moved through the sand. He was already consuming me.

Darkness fell and the castle grounds came to life with lamps glowing across the textured exteriors. I'd spent the afternoon roaming the city on foot, admiring frescoes painted with ground-up gemstones on the walls of streets and havelis. The silhouettes of women draped in vividly coloured saris gave the city a feeling of enchantment. A caravan of camels sauntered by me in a laneway, and as the call to prayer echoed off the ancient sandstone structures, I glimpsed a vision of life on the Silk Road during the rule of the Mughal Empire. As the vision morphed I remembered the man's eyes from earlier, looking at me through the desert haze, inky black and enticing. I wondered if our paths would cross again at the castle.

Dehydrated from walking the bone-dry streets, I wandered down to the bar to find a cold drink. Billing it to my room, I sipped the fresh watermelon and ginger juice, deciding to take a walk now the temperature was dropping. Approaching the Hindu shrine in the courtyard below my room, I lingered and watched the candles flickering in the low light of the evening. Offerings of marigold flowers glowed orange and yellow in the ambience of the flames. As I stood in the warm air of dusk in the desert, I felt that someone was watching me. Turning to inquire of my surroundings, I saw a man's figure standing near the entrance to the courtyard. Though my eyes couldn't see his, I knew it was the man from before.

Perhaps taking my steady gaze in his direction as an invitation, he began to walk towards me across the distance of the courtyard. Heat flushed in my face as I moved to the top of a stairway, deliberately, wanting to be found. I stood overlooking the lower courtyard with an elegantly designed pool and a view across the city of 50,000 people. He reached my side and halted. Smiled. *My name is Joaquin. And your name is?* We shared small talk under the sandstone archway before he invited me to sit on the cane daybeds by the pool. I listened, watched, transfixed. His voice was a song; the intonations of his accent flitting in my ears.

After sitting for some time, he asked if I'd like to take a walk around the castle. Entering different chambers, we marvelled at the architecture from the 1700s. Sprawling bougainvillea vines climbed the castle walls, green leaves exploding into bouquets of fuchsia that shimmered in the moonlight. Shadowy green palm fronds swayed in the breeze. Small grey squirrels that raced in brazen excitement across the lawns earlier in the day had retired for the night. We wandered through sandstone rotundas with elegant domed tops and shiny marble floors, before making our way back down to the glazed water of the pool.

Standing close to the upper courtyard wall, we were out of sight of any staff or guests who may have been enjoying the night air. As we stood, inches apart under a moon growing heavy towards fullness, we were fevered by the thrill of crossing paths in this offbeat city that was beyond the tourist corridor.

May I kiss you? He whispered, leaning in close.

Eyes locked. Bodies pulsating. There was a moment of hesitation before I reached out to feel the strength of his shoulder under my fingers. My hand moved down to the bicep pressing out of his linen and silk shirt, and my fingers gripped him tighter. My other hand met his, as our fingertips touched skin to skin. We pulled each other close as our bodies began to merge. The charge in the base of my spine was volcanic as I surrendered to his masculinity. He gripped me against the wall of the castle, our hands shaking and searching each other in the adrenaline of being caught. The saltiness of his dark skin in the desert air was tantalising. Our bodies rippled together, milk and masala chai under moonlight.

Taking a breath, we pulled ourselves from the intoxication and I told him I would see him again tomorrow if he wished. He walked me to my room and kissed me goodnight on the balcony in the dark. I fumbled the vintage bronze key into the lock and disappeared behind the heavy door. I fell asleep with a face as bright as the sun.

When my travels took me on to my next stop in Jaipur, a city of glistening gems and vibrantly patterned textiles, my lover would accompany me for a short stay in a haveli. The experience left me buzzing, breathless. A sense of spontaneity, lightness and sensuality that my heart hadn't felt for quite some time.

~

A week after the love affair I found myself on the river Ganges, drifting on the water in an old wooden boat. As we floated in the darkness the city was already writhing. Pilgrims bathed as crematory fires blazed along the banks, the flames reflecting on the surface of the murky black water. The air here was so thick with pollution it created a veil for my retinas, so I stared into the sun as it rose high above the horizon. As I gazed through the smoggy glare the entire scene felt otherworldly. I was, after all, in Varanasi – the holiest city in India. Where pilgrims come to die with the promise of liberation from saṃsāra, the endless cycle of suffering through life, death and rebirth.

The boat veered towards the bank and my eyes were drawn to the flame. Ash and smoke rose above and floated into the distance. One, two, three, four cloth-wrapped bodies were smouldering, under the rising sun on the bank of the river Ganges. Stepping a foot from the boat to the earth, a feeling of being forbidden swept over me. Surely I couldn't be here to see the sacred dissolving of these bodies into the ether – but my guide beckoned me on to witness the full ritual from ashore.

The smoke and ash drifted over me as the wind changed direction. It did not hold the stench of burning flesh as I had expected; the bodies adorned with fragrant flowers and sandalwood before being ignited. In the flames I saw my father. His life; fleeting, gone. So many lives. Hundreds of bodies burnt right here, every day. An offering to the gods and the Ganges. A supplication: *please – redeem us from this incarnation.*

I wept as I watched, cried at the mundane and the mystery of death – felt the ending we all move towards with each breath. Though when it comes, it will shatter us in the shock of our disbelief. It was written on the walls of our worlds all along. I'd waited for a clarity that never ever came. *It just is …* My heart whispered. *It all just is. Make of it what you will. The answers are not out there. They're always within. At the core of your being. You do not need to search, you do not need to wander. Just stop, sit, and go within yourself. You have this life to live, in pleasure and in pain, and you will expand through it all beyond the very edges of yourself.*

My back to the river, face towards the flames, I turned to the city high above the steps of the ghat. As I moved, climbing the stairs, I ascended into the swarming streets with a knowing no more certain than I'd had before. But in my uncertainty, I felt a steady peace. An acceptance.

It just is.

ZOE PERRY is an author, artist, creative arts therapist, and devoted mum, living on Awabakal and Worimi Lands in Newcastle, Australia. She holds a Bachelor of Politics and International Relations from the University of Canberra, along with further qualifications as a sound healer, Reiki practitioner, and in natural therapies and fitness, bringing a rich and multifaceted perspective to her life and work. Her career has been as colourful as her art – spanning disability support, dance teaching, and community services across alcohol and other drug, mental health, and homelessness. She has contracted to DFAT on Australia's aid and development programs, and worked as a probation and parole officer in corrective services. Zoe now works remotely for a not-for-profit and devotes herself to painting, writing, and facilitating workshops and ceremonies that help others heal and discover themselves through creativity. Her Substack, Surviving Adulthood, explores all things human and beyond - motherhood, relationships, spirituality, mental health, grief, and the big questions of life - with a touch of humour and her lively ADHD spark.

zoeperry.com.au | @zoe_creative_arts | @zoe_art_and_soul

ALWAYS WITH ME

ELIZABETH HAMMANG

For every parent with an angel in the stars,
and to those still waiting for their miracle.

I sat there in the unforgiving bathroom, eyes squeezed tightly shut, holding the pregnancy test in my shaking hands, bare feet planted on the cool tiles beneath me, completely terrified of what the result would mean for me and my family. Not what you would call the 'typical family', being made up of my husband, our four-year-old miracle daughter, and our nine angel babies living in the stars.

I took a deep breath, turned the test over in my hands, and opened my eyes ...

You see, a negative pregnancy test is something I am no stranger to, a result I have come to accept time and time again over the space of our twelve-year fertility journey. Don't get me wrong, seeing only one line is utterly heartbreaking and does not get any easier as time goes on, but at least I know in that moment where I stand. A brutal but honest truth.

A positive pregnancy test, on the other hand, is a result that comes with so much more complexity than I ever could have imagined at the beginning of this journey. A result that I've come to realise, more often than not, does not always end with a baby delivered safely in your arms. Not for me, and not for so many others.

I remember growing up and being taught in school that every time you even look at someone of the opposite sex you could end up pregnant. What I wasn't taught was that pregnancies can end, sometimes just as quickly as they began. Other times they can be dragged out for weeks or months on end, slowly breaking you down until you are nothing but a shell of your former self. They can make you lose faith in the health system, the ability of your family and friends to understand and support you, your compatibility with your partner, and most significantly, your body's ability to carry and nurture life. It can be incredibly isolating and so deeply confusing.

The two-week wait following ovulation has always been so triggering for me, a time that has really tested the patience of what some people around me would call an already very impatient woman. If I had a dollar for every time someone said to me during this time to 'just relax', 'try not to think about it' or 'at least you know you can get pregnant', then I might just be able to fund all the fertility treatments and medications I have had to endure over the years. Not even a drop in the ocean compared to other families. And whilst most of these comments might be said with no ill intention, unfortunately they only exacerbate the feelings of failure that I had already been living with. They have contributed to the dismissal of my experience, and they have invalidated the truth of my reality. I know I am not alone in feeling this way. Instead of teaching us that we will get pregnant every time we have sex, wouldn't it be more appropriate and more beneficial to teach us how to support someone who is struggling with their fertility or who has experienced the loss of a baby? Seems like a no-brainer to me.

People around me might say that I don't like surprises. I don't really believe this to be true. However, after experiencing such a tumultuous and exhausting time trying to bring a living baby home, I guess you could say that I do not enjoy being blindsided by the unknown, and for the sake of my sanity I need to be prepared for any potential outcome. Unfortunately, in the world of fertility and babies, this is just not an achievable scenario, and it is something I struggle with every single day. Even now, after twelve years on this journey, I have not experienced anywhere near the plethora of possibilities in this realm. It is simply infinite, and only after having undertaken my own research and hearing about the journeys of other people who exist in this space do I know this to be true. It is just not something you are taught when growing up. We spend our time sheltering the truth of what life can be just to avoid the awkwardness and uncomfortability of these conversations. I wish I had known. I wish I hadn't been so blindsided.

I wish I could tell you how many pregnancy tests I've taken over the years, but like many other people on a similar journey to mine, you simply lose count. Even if you see those two lines, one test is simply not enough. I would redo pregnancy tests at least three times a day just to see if there was any change in that second line or if it would even show up at all. Testing became the only thing I could control in an otherwise uncontrollable situation. I would sit there impatiently, counting down the seconds to confirm the result, eyes squinting to see if that second line would appear and if it would be lighter or darker than the previous test. Holding the test at so many different angles and in different levels of light all around the house, just praying a second line would magically appear. Checking with my husband to see if what I was seeing wasn't just a figment of my imagination. Sometimes this process would last a few days, the second line slowly appearing and then subsequently fading, confirming an early pregnancy loss. Other times it would last for weeks on end, blood tests and ultrasounds neither confirming nor denying a viable pregnancy, and on the very rare occasion it would leave me where I am right now, blessed to be growing a life, but riddled with anxiety, utterly terrified of losing another child.

Pregnancy after loss and infertility is a journey in and of itself. It is what I would call the ultimate showcase of the duality that exists within this human experience. You have so much gratitude and love for the miracle or miracles growing inside you, whilst constantly holding your breath, frozen with fear, terrified of what you could lose, all whilst knowing firsthand that it is a definite possibility. You know this because you have lived it before. It has been your reality. And in my experience, the people around you, more often than not, don't know what to do with this information. It is uncomfortable for them, and they don't know how to act around you.

If you are happy and excited all the time, then you are living in a fantasy world, in complete denial of what you have been through before. If you are anxious and depressed, hiding away from the world, then you aren't being grateful for your blessings and for the living child you already have. It is truly exhausting. But if I have learnt anything throughout my journey, it is that both things can be true. All these feelings can co-exist and that does not mean you are broken or ungrateful. It means you are human. It means that you have lived through one of the greatest losses that anyone can ever experience, nine times over, and you have survived.

Speaking of survival, this can look so vastly different for different people and can honestly change depending on the day of the week. For me, sometimes this looks like me filling my calendar with social activities, spending time laughing with my friends at the silliest things and just being outside of my home, away from that bathroom where everything can be taken from you in a single wipe. Other times, it is me curled up in bed or on the lounge with a book, holding my daughter against my heart, breathing in her light and pure magic, a place where I know I am the closest I can ever feel to my angel babies being with us. Some days this fills me with such gratitude and love for each and every one of my babies choosing me to be their mama, and on other days, it feels like I can barely make it through without my heart breaking into a million pieces. Both experiences can be real, and both can be true. I know this because I live it every single day.

In all honesty, and something I find quite difficult to admit, is that before I had experienced the loss of my babies, I didn't know why I was here in this life. I felt lost. I chopped and changed courses and careers, nothing ever feeling like it fit who I came here to be. I had so many ideas of what I should be doing, all so varied and not congruent with who I actually was at my core. A storyteller. A healer. I struggled to fit in with those around me and never felt like I was being understood or that I belonged. All I did know was that I wanted to help, but I never knew what that looked like.

As hard as losing a baby is, and it is incredibly hard, I do feel that it has ignited something deep within me. A deep need to share my story. To hold space for those who have gone through a similar experience. To spread awareness, education, and understanding of what it means to be on a fertility journey or experience pregnancy or baby loss. But most of all, to sprinkle the love I have for my babies and share it with the whole collective. To not let that love die with their physical vessels. To be the portal for their higher purpose and allow it to be rebirthed through all that I do in this life.

There is so much I could say when it comes to the experience someone like me has had, and yet no words feel quite enough for what the reality has been. I'm not sure I could ever truly convey just how much this has changed and shaped me. I have travelled to the absolute lowest places in my mind. I've felt trapped, I've felt useless, I've felt judged, I've felt guilty, I've felt alone, I've felt complete devastation and like I simply can't go on. Alongside all these true and valid feelings, I've also felt so much gratitude, so much joy, and so much hope. Picturing your baby's life begins the minute you see those two lines, however faint they might be, and just for that single moment, however brief it might be, I feel so unbelievably blessed.

Anniversaries are hard, so are Mother's Day, Father's Day, birthdays, and in some cases, your average Tuesday. But then again, some days are lighter and brighter than you thought they could be. Sitting here now, writing this the day after the one-year anniversary of the loss of our twin boys, what is surprising is how some days that feel like they should be the hardest, just aren't. I think I built up the day so much in my mind that I was so beyond prepared for all that I might feel, and the beautiful thing about yesterday was that I just felt so close to my babies, and so full of gratitude for them choosing me to be their mama.

I think what shocked me the most is that I didn't even cry. For someone who isn't afraid to shed tears most days, this took me by surprise. Instead, I held my babies at the forefront of my mind and thanked them for choosing me. Even if only for eleven weeks physically, I know I have them in my heart forever. Until we meet again. They give me so much purpose in this life, and for that alone I am truly grateful.

This is for them.

A year today since you both left my womb,
And it feels like just yesterday.
To be sitting here now, thirty-one weeks pregnant
With your baby sister.
Feeling her kicks, seeing her grow.

So unbelievably blessed, and yet
Beautifully bittersweet.

I wish it didn't, but I know now,
That it always had to be this way.
I did all I could for you in this life,
I know that you couldn't stay.
It still hurts though, just like it did that day.

And every day since, I think of you both,
Just like I do your brothers and sisters.
Knowing you really couldn't ever leave me completely.
Imprinted on my soul,
Etched deep within my body.

Forever.

And always with me.

ELIZABETH HAMMANG lives in Sydney with her husband, their four-year-old daughter and fur babies. She is also a mother to nine angel babies. A graduate of University with distinction, she holds a Bachelor of Health Science (Health Promotion). Elizabeth is an advocate for all areas of women's health, specifically around fertility and pregnancy loss awareness. An avid reader and book reviewer, you can connect with Elizabeth at @lizzies.little.library on Instagram, whether you'd like to talk about your favourite book or have a deeper conversation about women's health, her DMs are always open.

MISSING

KRISTINA GARLA

For Agatha Christie (the queen of mystery) and my younger self (who devoured her books).

'Mrs Harrison is missing.'

Kyla looked at her sister, Agnes, who was standing by the front door. She deliberately waited until she had walked up the path and was standing directly beside her sister before responding. 'What do you mean Mrs Harrison is missing?'

'Gone. And Isla is very upset. *Very* upset. And so am I.'

Noticing the flush in her sister's face, Kyla leaned towards her as she answered almost in a whisper, 'Well, that is no surprise, you are twins. You have always said you feel the same emotions.'

Agnes glared at her. 'Now isn't the time to be petty, Kyla.'

Kyla took a deep breath and reminded herself, as she often did when negotiating with her sister Agnes, that it is a *practice of patience*. With a sigh she said, 'OK, Agnes. It is 8.00 in the morning. I have had to drop the kids off to Perry's place and rush over here. I am going to be late for work. I am sure Mrs Harrison can't be far.'

'I called both you and Perry. Why isn't she here?'

'I don't think we need everyone here, Agnes, and someone has to look after our children for goodness' sake. Michael and Cameron are off together on a boys' trip. You know this.'

'We need everyone here to search for Mrs Harrison, and to talk to the police.'

'The police?'

'Yes, I rang them. Before I rang you.'

Kyla sat on the front porch chair and put her head in her hands for a moment. She brushed over her eyebrows with the tips of her fingers, a nervous childhood habit, and looked up as she started to say, 'Oh, Agnes, do you think that was …' Her words caught in her throat as the police car crunched over the gravel of the drive.

Two police officers stepped out. A woman and a man. Kyla squinted at them. The woman was much younger than the man. A seasoned cop and a rookie, she gathered.

Almost comically, they both straightened their caps at the same time as they stood up. The younger one, the woman, bent back into the car to retrieve her clipboard as the older policeman made his way towards Kyla and her sister Agnes. The young female police officer followed close behind, with tiny, rushed steps, trying to catch up. Kyla noticed her polished shoes glistening in the morning sun as she scurried up the path.

'Good morning, I'm Sergeant Hal and this 'ere is Constable Annabelle.'

Kyla thought the first-name basis odd but smiled as politely as she could as she stood up and extended her hand towards him. Sergeant Hal, oblivious to the invitation to shake hands, placed his hands on his hips, took a deep breath into his chest and then said to no one in particular, 'I believe a "Mrs Harrison" is missing?'

Constable Annabelle nodded in agreement behind him as she diligently wrote his words on her clipboard notepad.

'Yes, that is correct,' answered Agnes.

'OK, let's get some details.'

Sergeant Hal was wasting no time.

'When did you last see Mrs Harrison?'

'It was about 6.00 am, just as the sun was coming up. She was outside in the front garden, while I had a shower,' Agnes explained.

'Bit early to be in the front garden, ain't it?' Sergeant Hal stated rather than asked as he tilted his head toward Agnes.

'It was our routine.'

'I see. So what happened next?'

Agnes continued. 'Well, I got out of the shower four minutes later. I know how long exactly because I set a timer. I don't have much time to shower between looking after my sister Isla and Mrs Harrison. I walked out to get Mrs Harrison, but she was gone. Nowhere to be seen.'

'Is that unusual?'

'Well, of course it is, Sergeant, or I would not have called you,' snapped Agnes.

'I see.'

Kyla watched as Sergeant Hal nervously shifted his weight from one foot to the other, while his face coloured. Agnes had this effect on people. It didn't matter who you were in the community. She could look at you with those steel-blue eyes of hers and cut you down with a handful of words.

'What's your usual routine?' he continued after composing himself.

'Well, after my shower and Mrs Harrison's time in the garden, I collect her and we all have breakfast together. Usually on the front porch. Isla, Mrs Harrison and I have warm porridge. I heat it in the microwave. Those packet oats. They both love them. I serve it to them with a little bit of almond milk, as their stomachs can't tolerate dairy.'

'I see.'

Sergeant Hal paused for a moment and watched Constable Annabelle rushing to take down the conversation word for word.

'It's a nice morning, could she perhaps have gone for a walk?'

'Don't be ridiculous, Sergeant! She never leaves the front yard. Ever.'

'OK. So, let's see …' Sergeant Hal looked at his watch momentarily. 'Uh, this means she has been missing for about two and a half hours?'

'Yes.'

Kyla thought it must be a slow day at the police station that morning. She guessed in this small country town it was probably always slow. In the city, someone would have to be missing for days before the police took them seriously. Here, they came straightaway.

'I understand she's elderly?'

As Sergeant Hal asked the question, Kyla guessed this may have been another reason why these police officers left their toast and jam to go cold on their desks and rushed over. Although, looking at Sergeant Hal's shirt, she decided he had finished his toast in the car on the way here. The drip of jam drying in the morning sun on his collar was a clue.

'Yes, she is quite elderly,' answered Agnes. 'She has difficulty walking and is almost blind, which is why we are so worried.'

'Perhaps we can also talk to your sister Isla?' asked Sergeant Hal as he motioned towards the front door.

Kyla jumped in quickly before Agnes could answer. 'She won't be any help, Sergeant. She has dementia, and she sleeps late. She has also lost her ability to talk.'

Agnes glared at Kyla.

'I see,' said the Sergeant in reply as he watched the exchange between the sisters.

Kyla's stomach grumbled in protest at her missing breakfast. She smiled sheepishly at everyone.

'Does Mrs Harrison have dementia too?' asked the Sergeant.

'Of course not,' Agnes answered impatiently. 'What a ridiculous question.'

'Well, let's get a description of her. What colour hair?'

'White.'

'Eyes?'

'Dark brown.'

'What was she wearing?'

'A tartan vest.'

'I see.'

They stood without talking for a moment, the scratching of Constable Annabelle's pen on paper filling the silence.

'Do you have a picture of her then?' the Sergeant asked.

As Agnes went inside the house to retrieve one, the Sergeant announced to no one in particular, 'We'll have a little look around.'

Kyla watched as Constable Annabelle clipped her pen to her clipboard and followed the Sergeant wherever he went in the front yard. Looking closely at the ground, Constable Annabelle bent down near the bush beside the front gate. She was staring intently at something. Reaching into her back pocket, she pulled out a snap-lock bag and a pair of tweezers and put the object inside. Kyla felt her chest tighten. She watched as the Constable walked up to the Sergeant and showed him what she had collected. They walked back to Kyla on the front porch and arrived in front of her at the same time Agnes came outside with a photo in her hand.

'Does anyone who lives here smoke cigarettes?' the Sergeant asked, directing his question to Agnes who he now understood to be the one in charge of this house.

'No, we do not. A disgusting habit.'

Agnes looked at the bag and then looked at Kyla.

'I knew it,' she said. 'I knew you had something to do with this.'

Kyla turned her head to Agnes. 'What *are* you talking about?' she asked, her voice a little shaky.

'Oh, you know. You have been wanting to be rid of Mrs Harrison for some time now. So you and Perry can put in place your plan for Isla to go into a nursing home. You know she won't leave Mrs Harrison. So you took her away. Where is she?'

Sergeant Hal and Constable Annabelle were statues. Their eyes were the only things moving, darting from sister to sister during the exchange.

Kyla turned to the Sergeant and addressed him.

'You will have to excuse my sister. She's a little overwhelmed and tired from looking after our sister, her twin. She has cared for her for many years as Isla's health has deteriorated. Agnes becomes a little … delusional … when tired. Not to mention … unreasonable. Yes, I smoke cigarettes, that much is true. But I haven't been here in weeks up until this morning when I was summoned. It is, of course, possible that when I was leaving last time, I dropped the butt of my cigarette there at the gate and …'

'Don't insult our intelligence!' interrupted Agnes, her voice rising. 'Nor our efforts to keep this house spotless. I would never have left your cigarette butt there for weeks, Kyla. Admit it. You have killed Mrs Harrison haven't you!'

'How dare you …' yelled Kyla, raising her arms and clenching her fists.

'OK now, let's everyone calm down,' said the Sergeant, stepping between the sisters.

Turning to Agnes he said, 'These are serious allegations you make. Let's start with you giving us a look at that photo and we'll go for a drive around the block and see if we can locate Mrs Harrison. Sometimes the elderly, they wander off a little. We see it all the time. Hopefully she won't be too far, and we'll bring her back to you before lunch.'

He took the photo from Agnes before she could answer.

The Sergeant closed his eyes and sighed.

'I see,' he said, without opening them. He pursed his lips and then handed the photo to Constable Annabelle, blinking his eyes open in the sun as he did so.

Constable Annabelle looked at the photo and then back at the Sergeant, her eyes full of surprise.

'Mrs Harrison is a … Scottish terrier? A dog?' Sergeant Hal's eyebrows raised and then his eyes squinted a little as he asked this question, looking directly at Agnes.

'Yes!' she screamed with exasperation. 'Of course she is! What else would she be? And *she* killed her!'

Agnes was pointing at Kyla. And then she wasn't. To everyone's surprise, Agnes pushed Sergeant Hal to the side and launched at her sister, knocking her to the ground.

'Where is she?! Where is Mrs Harrison?!' she screamed repetitively as she punched her sister in the chest while pinning her to the ground with her knees.

Constable Annabelle dropped her clipboard and pen, along with the photo of Mrs Harrison, on the ground. She immediately went to the aid of her superior, helping Sergeant Hal stand once again. He had fallen onto his back after losing balance, caught off guard by the ferocity of Agnes's shove and her surprising strength. Together,

Constable Annabelle and Sergeant Hal tried to remove Agnes off Kyla and restrain her. It took great effort as the wildness inside her was unpredictable and a force they were not expecting.

It took some time, but they managed it. Eventually, they placed Agnes in the back of the police car to contain her. She sat there glaring at Kyla and Sergeant Hal, while Constable Annabelle sat beside her, looking a little shaken by it all and quite dishevelled compared to how she arrived.

The sun won't be glistening off those shoes no more thought Kyla.

Sergeant Hal picked up the clipboard from the front lawn, along with Constable Annabelle's pen and cap, his cap and the photo of Mrs Harrison.

'We'll go for a drive around the block and see if we can locate the dog.'

He took out a crisp white handkerchief from his pocket and wiped the dirt and sweat from his face.

'Then we'll take your sister to the station and give her a cuppa, to settle her down a bit.'

He placed his police cap on his head and straightened his posture as he straightened his cap.

Kyla gave him a cool look.

'I would like to press charges. Assault.'

Sergeant Hal brushed the dirt from his pants. He looked at Kyla with sadness in his eyes. A sadness which reached the edges of his voice as he answered, 'Sure thing, we'll write up a report.'

Kyla watched him walk back to his car. As he sat down in the driver's seat, he said something to Constable Annabelle and Agnes. Kyla could not hear what it was, but she could tell from the look on their faces and the way they stared at her as the car pulled away that he had informed them of her wishes.

Licking the blood from her gums, Kyla picked up her phone from the path. Inspecting it for scratches and damage for a moment, she dialled the last number she had called earlier that morning.

'Darling sister Perry,' she said, 'it all went to plan. You can contact the nursing home and let them know we want to take that place for Isla.'

There was silence for a moment on the line, and then Perry answered.

'I already have. I emailed them early this morning when you were burying the dog.'

'Great. Although perhaps you should have waited in case the cops go snooping. Not that I think they would be smart enough to work it out.'

Kyla turned to face the house as she said this. Staring at her from the bedroom window was Isla. She was gripping her walker and looking directly at Kyla.

'I know what you did,' she mouthed silently at Kyla. 'I saw you.'

It was at that very moment from across the street that a Mr Jenkins nearly choked on his butter-soaked crumpet as he watched Kyla from his kitchen window. He gasped as he saw her drop her phone and hit her head hard on the ground as she fainted.

KRISTINA GARLA is a writer, speaker and coach whose work lies at the intersection of linguistics, literature and living. She explores the role of language and storytelling in shaping culture and the human experience, with particular interest in soma-linguistics, etymology and archetypal theory. Her focus is on understanding how narrative and recurring patterns within the collective conscious influence behaviour, and how positive affirmations and the Buddhist principle of Right Speech can modify gene activity and neuroplasticity. Kristina's fascination with mystery began in childhood through reading Agatha Christie novels and deepened during her Bachelor of Arts, majoring in Linguistics and Literature, where she engaged with classical literature, philosophy and the great thinkers. Over time, this love of mystery expanded into a spiritual lens, inspired by Buddhist texts, the yoga sutras and philosophy. Her work has been published in anthologies and magazines, and she is a regular blogger. Through her writing, Kristina peacefully insists on truth and trusts in the guidance of love to change the world.

kristinagarla.com

DON'T FALL IN LOVE WITH ME, I WRITE POETRY

S. A. SISIKA

To Beth, Clay and Rena, thank you for being a part of the whimsy and the chaos. My writing journey would not have been the same without you cheering me on every step of the way.

Don't fall in love with me,
I write poetry.
I'll take your beating heart and make it bleed,
Without you even knowing.
I'll take your darkest parts,
Shine a light on them and call it art,
Just to remind you, you're only human.

I'll write about your grief and how you can't sleep.
I'll write about the butterflies, the joy, the anxiety.
I'll write about the sound of your voice, the colour of your eyes
and what they do to me.
I'll write about the curve of your lips,
The shape of that birthmark on your rib,
I'll wear my heart on my sleeve for the whole world to see,
I'll put it all in print and frame it to hang in the halls of history,
People will stand in awe and say,

'I can never tell what he was feeling,
But she really loved him, didn't she?
What a lonely existence that would have been.'
They'll walk away feeling like a part of them has finally been seen,
Like that unrequited love they had at twenty-three,
The one that didn't make sense and felt like a fever dream,
One where they can still remember every taste, touch and sound so vividly.

These are the moments that I live for,
The legacy that I want to leave,
You see,
I tragically worship the human existence,
And I must write about the human experience mentally, emotionally, and spiritually,
So please,
Don't fall in love with me,
If you don't want to become poetry.

THE SEVEN WONDERS OF RUNNING FROM YOURSELF

S. A. SISIKA

Maybe you didn't realise it,
But,
Maybe your body was an escape for someone once.
I know my body has been,
A safe haven,
A familiar playground for someone to come running back to,
When everything else in life was going wrong.
My body was once a temple to worship at,
To pray that better days would come,
And when they did,
My body was no longer the sweet solace, the peaceful paradise in a cruel world,
It became an empty palace,
Abandoned ruins of promises for something beautiful,
A wonder to stand in awe of but never feel the need to come back to,
My body used to mean everything to someone,
Once.

S. A. SISIKA is an emerging Papuan-Australian poetry and novel writer based on Ngunnawal and Ngambri Country/ Canberra. Through her writing, S. A. Sisika aims to tap into emotions which lurk beneath the surface, waiting to be spoken to. Her writing explores love, friendship, relationships, self-discovery, identity, and emotional truths. She hopes to empower readers to explore the deepest parts of themselves and to express their inner worlds.

@tealeavesandbiblichor

THE BOY ON THE BEACH

JACQUI DOYLE

My feet drop into the soft sand as I step from the hot cement onto the beach. As I walk, the sand squeaks under my feet. It flicks up and hits the backs of my legs. As I make my way down to the harder sand by the water's edge, I search for a breeze. I long for the coolness to push the day into the peripheries of my mind as I let it settle like sand in water. Tommy runs past me, head jutting forward like a seagull staking a claim over a wayward chip. Arms stretched backwards from his body like thrusters from an imagined superhero suit. His thick brown hair, that is curly when long, and straight when kept short like now, bends back reluctantly from his forehead from the rush of movement. Not from the wind. There is no breeze today.

We turn right once we reach the water's edge and walk towards the headland of Point Perry. The rocks reflect the golden sunlight of the late afternoon, and it makes them look like a mosaic of different shades of orange and beige. Tommy stops at the bottom of the first mound of rocks and looks back at me.

'Can you help me climb, Mummy?'

'You're right, mate. You have a go, and I'll help you if you need me. I'll be right here.'

He is five. Just. Big for his age. People always assume he's seven and try to speak to him as such. He likes people, both adults and children, but he is only five. He'll talk your head off once he gets used to you, and about quite a range of subjects – school, dinosaurs, cricket, his friends even if you don't know them. He's physically adept, and I encourage him to be so because life is easier when you are. You can participate more, get involved in things more easily, feel like you fit in.

He's half-way up the rocks, picking his way slowly up the face of the mound. It's not steep, but it's challenging for inexperienced feet and ankles.

He's my only one. Will only ever be. Not my decision. My body's decision, maybe. My husband's body's decision, maybe, but no-one ever talks about it being their fault, do they? As women, we shoulder all that responsibility. Nobody stops us, mind you. We get to be devastated every month when it feels like our bodies betray us.

'Mummy, help!'

He's trying to go up a steep part when there is a much gentler route just to his right.

'Hey buddy, why don't you try moving over this way just a little bit? Move that foot … no, the other one … no, put that one down. That's it. Now lift your other foot … that's it! Move it over into that little hidey-hole. That's it, then move up that way.'

I was late to the party, I suppose. I got married in my late thirties, but it had never occurred to me that I might be leaving it too late for kids. My lineage's experience of motherhood was complicated. It was an expectation, a duty. It also cost you a lot to be a mother back then. It could be a burden. *Was that why I waited?* This thought had come to me on so many sleepless nights.

We had tried for quite a while before finally saying we could be happy without any kids at all. I remember making that decision and the sheer weight that left my shoulders in the moment. Within three months, I was pregnant. A gift. My most precious.

'Look at me, Mummy!'

He's at the top of the rocks, teetering to stand up to show me his accomplishment. I look at him and smile widely like only he can make me smile. The gappy grin created last Easter due to a small but unfortunate hiking accident makes my heart swell, always.

'Come up, Mummy! Have you seen what's over here?'

We've lived around the beach for the last eight years, so yes, I most probably have. I climb up the rock and look at the gap between two mounds of rock that he is looking at. It makes a miniature ravine with sand in the middle where the waves are still rushing up periodically. It does look pretty interesting this afternoon to be fair. There are a number of green crabs still sitting on the rocks in full view.

The pregnancy was pretty easy, really. I was hot all the time and had indigestion for six months, but other than that, I had had quite a trouble-free pregnancy and given birth naturally to a monstrous and very healthy baby boy. Given all this, obviously I could have another, right? I could grow and give birth to a very healthy baby once, so surely I could do it again.

He jumped onto the sand in the middle of the ravine with a 'Roooooaaaarrrrrrrr!' The green crabs scuttled into their respective hidey-holes. He giggled.

Obviously, the answer had been 'No'. It didn't happen again. On my forty-sixth birthday, I decided I should stop hoping. I needed to give myself the gift of not being devastated every month. I was not prepared for the grief that came with that. It hit me like a tidal wave, not letting me come up for air. I couldn't breathe, and yet I had to keep doing life. I had to keep being Mum. I had to keep going to work. I had to keep all the commitments I was prone to making. My husband meanwhile couldn't understand why I couldn't be happy with what we had. Neither could I. Not only was I grieving, but I was ashamed of this grief.

There was an older boy and his mum inspecting something further down the miniature ravine. Tommy sauntered up and asked what they were looking at. They told him and showed him whatever it was. I was outside the ravine, meandering on the other side of the rocks and couldn't hear. Satisfied with their explanation, Tommy kept wandering down to the opening in the rocks and out towards me. Suddenly he turned and started climbing the rocks to the side. He still had his school uniform on, but bare feet. His collar was done all the way up, as Sebastian in Grade Six likes to do it. Tommy thinks Sebastian is pretty cool, so that's how he likes his collar too.

I don't take many photos. Even though my phone is usually pretty close by, I just never think to take it out. With the light the way it was that afternoon, it did occur to me. I took a number of shots, but my favourite was where he was a bit blurry. A boy, on the sand, deep in investigation mode. Moss-covered rocks, some with barnacles, on either side and a not quite overcast, but certainly cloudy sky in the background.

This is how I see him. By himself. He will never be a brother, an uncle. He will never have a sibling or a niece or nephew. The grief isn't just for me. For the mother of multiple kids I will never be, the noisy home I will never have. It is also for him. For the things he will never experience as a consequence. In those moments, I feel the most like a failure. When I feel the most fucking angry. When I feel the most everything.

Tommy suddenly comes running up to me, his face glowing with joy and fresh air. I think he's coming in for a hug, and I brace myself for the thirty kilograms of boy that is about to smack into my midriff. At the last minute, he sidesteps me and rushes headlong into the water. It splashes up around him and onto his torso with a flurry of legs and white water. He then suddenly trips and ends up all but submerged under an incoming wave. He turns over and looks back at me laughing, his eyes shining in the light. *Ugh, no spare clothes,* I think to myself. And then I think, *Who fucking cares!*

I run into the water past him and feel the salty water hit my face. I get to knee depth and drop down onto my belly in a wave, my linen top and shorts feeling immediately heavy in the water.

I turn and shout, 'You coming in or what!'

He squeals with excitement and jumps onto his feet and rushes headlong up to where I am being buffeted by waves on my belly. Tommy jumps onto my back and splashes water all around my face. I turn and wrap him up in a bear hug so that he can't use his arms to splash me anymore. He roars with playful rage. I'm still stronger than him. For now.

Whoever said 'time heals all' and 'everything happens for a reason' was an idiot. You don't forget. You don't suddenly think that your life is so much better because of that life-altering thing that happened to you. Perhaps it will get easier to carry with time. It still feels very heavy. Awkward to carry, and without solid form, I stumble trying to keep it from landing on someone around me. It is, after all, only mine. I don't want to burden others with it, and so if it spills out, I am always ashamed. There are moments when it feels easier. Maybe one day it will feel easier more often. But I also know that I will always carry this sadness with me in the moments I have the space to let it in.

As we walk off the beach onto the hard cement, Tommy says, 'That was fun, Mummy.'

I smile at him and say, 'Yeah, I really enjoyed that too, buddy.'

He looks at me with a serious look on his face and says, 'Can we have sushi on the way home? Pleeeeaaasse! Oh … can I watch

Fireman Sam at home? No, hang on, maybe Octonauts … nah, definitely Fireman Sam.'

'When he hears that fire alarm …' He starts to skip up the footpath ahead of me, singing at top note, oblivious to the looks from passersby.

JACQUI DOYLE and her family call Yandina on Queensland's Sunshine Coast home, where they enjoy the best of both worlds: the beautiful south-east coastline and one of Australia's most important food-growing regions. An interest in growing her own vegetables and living a more local, sustainable life inspired Jacqui to share her personal journey through writing. What began as a simple newsletter for friends – filled with the ramblings of a self-proclaimed 'lazy gardener' – soon revealed a natural talent for storytelling. Today, she writes about gardening, sustainability, and finding beauty in everyday life, hoping to inspire others to create their own little patch of loveliness.

jacqsbackyard.com | YouTube: Jacq's Backyard | @jacqs_backyard

CONFLOSUNDERATION

DONNA WALSH

To my daughter Bret for her beautiful heart, love, support and inspiration. To SOVU and my stage crew, you are the friends I never knew I needed and now can't imagine a life without you all in it. To our Dancing Queen, Melinda, thank you for your love, your curiosity, your insights, your encouragement and our memories. I wish we had had more steps.

Conflosunderation: a mixed word of confused, floating, sunder (split apart)

I made up the word 'conflosunderation' to try to describe a feeling. It's a suddenness. The shock when a loved one dies without much warning and time to prepare. It made me feel like I was floating and not part of this world. Like a vacuum. I have heard it could be dis-association or depersonalisation, yet that doesn't describe the feeling or emotion for what I was going through, or the complexity of it all. The numbness, disbelief, confusion, incomprehension, overwhelm, detachment, discombobulation, fracturing, the what-the-f – s and all that is between. For me, the word shock just doesn't cover it, and it doesn't quite reach grief yet. It isn't temporarily losing a grasp on reality because I knew it was real. It's in those moments before the anguish. I say moments, but it feels like an eternity.

I thought I was okay with grief and loss. I thought I had experienced and seen enough of it in my fifty-five years to be able to process pain, emptiness and the heart-wrenching void that it leaves. After all, I had lost my mother when I was twenty-four, eight months into my pregnancy. She was only fifty-two. To think that all those years ago, my mum woke up for the last time. It wasn't totally unexpected given the circumstances, but had she truly known it was her last day, what would she have said or done? It still feels strange to think it's been so long since we spoke or saw each other. I lost a mother as I was about to become one. It was a hard time, but I am so very grateful as it became a time of exceptional growth. It taught me so much. Especially around forgiveness, compassion, empathy and kindness. I look back now and know that it made me part of who I am. I continue to grow and evolve, this is all part of my journey. I am the mother I am because of that experience.

I thought, I have seen friends lose their children, their grandchildren, their brothers, their sisters, partners, parents and closest friends. All of it so tragic, often suddenly, sometimes a long journey, sometimes senseless, sometimes a relief.

And as a friend often said, 'You know what thought thought? Thought thought they fell out of bed, so they got out and had a look.'

I thought I was OK.

Until I wasn't. I couldn't make the story up if I tried.

I hadn't seen this remarkable woman in thirty years. Back then, we were more acquaintances than friends. In typical fashion, she organised a group of us from way back to get together. Not just a lunch or a coffee. No. We had a thirty-kilometre trek along mostly sand to raise money while we did it. I've never felt like I fit in, get very anxious and end up not going to events. But this one I thought I could do. I had a strategy if it got awkward, and I could always walk alone if needed. I should never have worried. She made me feel so seen. She made everyone feel seen. She really saw me. Saw through my masks and we connected. We were different people, but we worked. Bonded over our curious and frantic minds. It was safe to be me, in all my neurodivergent glory. This event also connected me with other women who I absolutely love and value, even if I hadn't seen some of them in a while.

She was always helping, organising and volunteering for many causes. She was many things to many people, and I loved her. We all loved her. When she needed us, we gathered around to help and support her in any way we could. One night, all of us got together and listened to each other tell hilarious stories, some about early dinner dates, or remote-control vibrating underpants. We'd all be hyperventilating with laughter.

As time went on, I caught up with her more regularly. Another night we danced, laughed and got to know each other more, and that night SOVU was truly born. *The Sisterhood of Vibrating Underpants.*

I felt as though I belonged. We all did. SOVU got together as often as our collective time allowed. We built new memories while reminiscing about our teenage years by the ocean. *'The Boys of Summer'* our theme song. My sunflower friends. It was like small seeds were planted and sprinkled with unconditional love. Fierce, connected, accepting love. We were an eclectic mix of varieties. Not the usual companions I've had, but beautifully honest, raw and real. In each other, we found new things. Like sunflowers, we faced each other when things got hard. In the mist, we were beside each other, not clearing the path but down in the weeds. Together, shining what light we could. Helping each other find our own way through. In the sunshine, we blossomed. Each individual their own ray of sunlight, making each other's world brighter by just being in it.

When the coronavirus and lockdowns were still a thing, we managed quite a few fiftieth parties and get-togethers, with tambourines and maracas a constant presence. We even managed a reunion by the ocean. We celebrated my fiftieth when I turned fifty-one. She spoke such eloquent, heartfelt and kind words I'll never forget. I was called the warrior woman, yet our dancing queen was the true warrior. I listened about the card given to me and how they say the average person walks 115 thousand miles in their life, and with me that was simply not enough.

'Sometimes you need people and fifty years or 100 years is not enough to be able to walk the planet with them. You are that girl. It's not enough. 200 years, 300 years wouldn't be enough for me.'

We definitely did not get enough steps.

It was inspiring to watch her transformation through grief. She was going to be OK. We even had an enlightening adventure to a local adult store. Learnt all about different tools and tricks. The special bag affectionately known as the doorstop. I had become *that friend*. To truly understand, Google 'Urzila Carlson Find a Friend'. Little did I know how true that would become.

In another lockdown, we spoke through her window. She looked dreadfully unwell, had lost weight rapidly and her colour was different. I knew something wasn't right. Only one doctor would see her. He could tell something wasn't right.

Leukaemia … an emergency now. Followed by another lockdown with no hospital visitation. I can still remember that conflosunderation. I felt so helpless. On the floor in the foetal position, heaving my weight in tears. Not knowing what to do really, I jumped to action and set up a Facebook help group for support. She was so stoic, always more worried about others than herself. For those who are wondering, I did retrieve the doorstop.

Acute myeloid leukaemia. Pretty shit by all accounts. Enduring month-long hospital stays and multiple rounds of chemo, each one more taxing than the last. With very few weeks between stays to recover at home and try to enjoy what little freedom was left, we took advantage of every moment.

When I held her hand, I'd tell her she had a choice. I let her know that it was OK to let go but also told her I'm pretty sure we had more steps. We were preparing for the worst. Eight months later, the call came, and the most beautiful word to hear was 'remission'. While I was so happy and relieved, I still had a gnawing feeling in the bottom of my gut. I was right. A brutal relapse occurred. As bad and horrific as it was, there was still hope.

Until the call, 'It's terminal.'

Eighteen months after that first call, it just felt unfair. There was no space between to really squeeze the juice out of life. This encouraged me to write again. She loved my words. It has helped me process the pain. My grief was palpable. Too much for some. Too big for me at times. Our small group of women all suffered, and while we supported each other for a time, we also drifted apart for a while.

When my body literally hijacked me, they were there. They'd been there all along, waiting in the wings. My stage crew. The ones that rally around without me asking, jump in and deal with things I didn't even know needed attention. Like a weighted blanket. Safe, secure, snug, serene and still. Like the comfort of a hot tea sipped from the cup with the perfect lip. No words. No platitudes. No shoulds. No if I was you. No problem solving. Just acceptance, listening, being, acknowledging. Just love. Shining the lights on my stage. Big, fierce, protective love. Manoeuvring the lights to help me find my way through the production, the show, the roller-coaster, the adventure that is … my life right now.

Even with support, I still couldn't understand why after almost a year I was still in so much pain. Then throw in menopausal rages and my whole body and mind becoming alien. Panic attacks. Darkness. Little joy. Feeling isolated. Feeling unworthy. Feeling mostly alone. So, I took the leap and went to therapy. In my mind, I had been doing all the right things. Eating healthy, exercising, meditating, journalling, writing poetry. But this time it just wasn't enough.

My first session, I nearly didn't walk through the door. I'm so glad I did. It was a huge lightbulb moment. After a series of deep questioning, I realised I'd lost one of my safe people and that I was in fear of losing people who provide me safety. Safe for me to be me, all of me, in my sometimes-sparkling rainbow unicorn mode or my quietly reflective recluse mode.

I began to understand that my grief and fear were not individual but compounded. A bit like a passenger train that's chugging along fine, hauling all the grief carriages along, not really taking notice of the load or the fuel being used. When the carriages are full, instead of emptying some out, I just added more carriages. This last carriage had the tracks shaking. The derailment was cataclysmic. Carriages concertinaed, some ripped in half. Some unrecognisable. All mixed up and compounded. Much repair was needed. My engine will never be the same, and I can no longer haul the same load. When I pull up at Therapy Station to let passengers off, some others still wait to get on. I need regular maintenance and reminders to stay on the tracks so I don't overload again.

I get it now. I mean really get it. How grief is often described as an ocean. It is vast and isolating. You're adrift, with no land or solid ground in sight. A never-ending body of water that wraps itself around you. It can be tumultuous, thrashing and frightening. It can be calm and quiet, almost tranquil. You can be floating on it, catching waves on it, swimming through it, treading water or drowning in it. Friends are like life rafts, appearing suddenly and saving you when the threat of going under is very real. Others are like lighthouses, a safety beacon when you are close to the edge. Always there, always shining some light.

And then after months, even years of being lost at sea, you sight land. It's still not quite in reach. It comes in and out of view until eventually you are close to shore. Suddenly a rip gets hold of you, and you are back out to sea. But now you have a little more hope that you'll see land again. Your confidence increases and you feel more at ease in this vast space. You know it's not forever. You're like a dolphin gliding through it now. Even playing in it. There's a pod around you and you are not alone.

One day, you wake up on the sand. Solid ground feels strange. You are drawn back and paddle in the shallows often. Occasionally, you venture out further, but this time you have the tools to get you back safely, like a surfboard riding those waves of grief. The surf can be huge and crushing, or the water can be like glass and it's in this moment you quietly paddle.

Either way, this is now part of who you are. You travel forward with this ocean. It's now part of your essence. You are now gaining strength from it. Over your lifetime, you become an accomplished surfer, paddler and swimmer. You cannot change the ocean or the tides for they will always be there, but you can flow with them.

I am now entering flow mode. Surfboard under my arm.

DONNA WALSH spent her formative years near the ocean on Butchulla country with gratitude and respect for K'Gari. Nature is her church. Initially wanting to be a journalist Donna switched her focus to environmental conservation and education after seeing the protests to save the Franklin River in Lutruwita (Tasmania) and hearing the Goanna song 'Let the Franklin Flow'. She did eventually get her journalism experience as Ranger Donna – a regular reporter for the children's TV show Totally Wild. Donna has always had a deep love for words. Real, heartfelt, moving words.

GRIEF AND THE PROTECTIVE HEART

STACEY HOWES

Dedicated to Ron Howes, my Dad, my hero.

I withheld my love, believing it was a form of protection. Underneath the hurt, misunderstandings, accusations, assumptions, outbursts, expectations and grief, the warm embers of love for you remained. My grief was wild and raw, driving me into survival mode. It was in that place of survival that I functioned, and I poured my whole heart and soul into being what I felt my mother needed, as she faced the end of her beautiful, impactful life.

Within the darkness of grief, those embers could not be extinguished.

From the day my mother was diagnosed with terminal cancer, I've carried my wounded heart like a fragile shield. I could see only my own version of grief. Only one way forward. I told myself I was open to other's perspectives, but looking back, through the lens of grief, I can see I really wasn't.

I couldn't see it then, how grief might take a different shape for others. How it might mean something else in their own relationship with Mum. All I could see was my inner child. Little Stacey. Watching my mother, my lifeline, my compass, my safe place, slip away from me and my children. I wasn't ready. I couldn't imagine our lives without her. The hurt was deep. The fear was overwhelming. And underneath it all, a desperate need to give her everything I could before she left. So, I held on and focused on what I thought was best. As if somehow that could keep her here a little longer.

The heartache of Mum's terminal diagnosis tore through our large, expansive family and lifelong friends, both of whom stretch across generations and locations. The devastation hit in waves over the following months and even more so after Mum took her last breath. We each knew Mum in our own way, having our own unique connections with her. She was a voice of reason, a moral compass, a comforter, a mediator, a nurturer, unshakeable in her love and the one who remembered the details no one else thought to hold. Without ever trying to control, she guided. Without demanding attention, she anchored us. Her heart was deep, full and intentional. She loved us as we were, never asking for more than our presence. She helped in practical ways, dropping things in, remembering what we needed before we asked and she loved to treat us, in both small and generous ways. She believed in making the most of life's opportunities, always encouraging growth and learning, and she shared her passions and her bright, positive energy with us – eager to see us thrive.

In the months that followed Mum's diagnosis, some of the tight-knit relationships we all once had began to be affected. Slowly, the tension became more apparent as the days went by and Mum's health deteriorated further. The slow but deeply felt decline in her ability to actively connect and bring reconciliation where needed, echoed across some relationships where we were at a loss of how to move forward without her gentle guidance. And over time, I truly grasped the understanding that she was 'the glue'. Yes, the glue that held us all together. The very essence of who she was.

Mum overcame many obstacles in her life and was driven to help anyone she sensed she could support. These challenges included ongoing systemic racism and single motherhood. Mum used her lived experience and intuition to support others meaningfully. She was the knowledge seeker and knowledge holder, and she was the first in our family to achieve a tertiary qualification and become a registered professional. She was there for us all, at any time, via text, phone calls, visits. Her personal networks were vast and crossed over to different cities and countries. Her professional impact was great as she worked with many organisations in her career to help bring systemic change and equity. She was a heart-led woman of true integrity and still, years after her death, I meet people who tell me how Mum impacted their lives. The professional mentorship she gave, the strong advocating she did for impactful change, helping families through trauma, connecting people to much needed and life-changing support services.

She was a special kind of 'glue'. She had warmth and patience as she navigated complex emotions with grace, understanding and compassion to help mend bridges, and bring healing to misunderstandings. She was 'home' to many of us. She was a prominent figure amongst us, who kept us grounded and connected to the core of who we are. She reminded us of who we are when at times, we didn't know and had lost our way. She was a pillar, which some of us were closer to than others, but still a solid, important presence and an enduring part of the family landscape, shaping who we were, even when she wasn't always at the centre.

So, when Mum was diagnosed, something in me shifted, and it marked the beginning of an unravelling I couldn't yet name. It not only triggered the deep grief for Mum that her life was ending and the fear for myself of how mine and my children's life would be without her, but it also triggered the fear of not knowing how to navigate through Mum's final days. I longed for guidance, but the one person I would usually turn to was the one who needed my strength.

Without having the awareness yet to understand the impact that Mum's diagnosis would have on others that loved her, my own expectations of how things should be began to arise. I cleared all my plans and dedicated everything I had to ensure Mum's final days on earth were what she wanted them to be. I expected a similar response from loved ones – but in a way that mirrored my own intensity. My deep, intrinsic desperation and grief pushed me into a state of high alert and panic. Panic to get everything right, or as close as possible. Intertwined, and at the heart of my desperate intensity, was love. And as my survival instincts kicked in, my focus narrowed only on Mum. Mum and my babies.

I reflect back on those days when the horror of losing Mum was becoming clearer. I long to have the ability to go back in time and to have understood things differently, and to have been more open to seeing each other's grief for what it was. To have been open to our own unique reactions and responses. To have put aside the considerations of whether someone's actions were right or wrong. To have had the deeper understanding that I do now, that there really are no right or wrong ways to respond to grief because grief is hard. Grief can be life-altering and at times, life-destroying. Grief changes people. Sometimes grief unites us and sometimes it divides us. And it is through my own unravelling after my mother died and journeying through my own darkness that I see my soul and I see my heart. And that underneath all my raw emotions, I just wanted her to live. The deepest part of me could not accept that we would no longer be together. Our kindred spirits. I could not make sense of this at the time because it was not a conscious thought, but a deep ache of devastation.

In the months before Mum died, the strain on some relationships grew, and bonds had become stressed and fragile. It was a hard time, and I know that it is not how any one of us wanted it to be. But in the midst of intense trauma that will change the lives of many people in different ways, we can experience inner turmoil where our mental clarity is affected, and have raw emotions of anger, fear, despair, overwhelm, sadness, helplessness, guilt and confusion when we lose or are losing a sense of stability. We can also be emotionally numb.

I felt all these things before and after Mum died, and to varying degrees. I also felt white-hot anger. Some of it was from the expectations and assumptions I had placed on some loved ones. But in reality, the fierce anger was because she lost her life and I lost her. The year after Mum died, I joined a grief group. This became a vital step in healing, and within the group, we shared the raw, unfiltered experiences of grief. In these gatherings of grieving hearts, I found space to express and release my anger alongside others who carried similar feelings, creating a shared understanding that eased the burden we all felt.

As I embraced my own personal reactions and responses to Mum's death, I realised that every other single person affected by Mum's death also had their distinct reactions and responses, too. Each of our experiences holds its own validity and truth, because the reality is that there is no one truth. We each experienced Mum's passing from our own angle of seeing the events unfold, coupled with our own unique make-up, past experiences and values. And at the heart of our actions was a desire to do what we felt was the right thing.

Most relationships that had become fractured, had naturally healed after Mum died. Even the most strained ones saw the anger and blame vanish almost instantly, with rapid and genuine heartfelt apologies. And to this day, those relationships remain stronger than they have ever been. Other relationships were mended, not with spoken words but with a quiet understanding of the souls where we both knew that it was grief that had caused us to show hurt sides of ourselves that were out of character.

Even so, in the months following Mum's passing, some relationships that had not previously been affected became painfully fraught. Some without an obvious catalyst while others became seeped in heartache, confusion and hurt, as the overwhelm of grief intensified. They were the darkest of days, and I held on to the hurt as renewed feelings of grief washed over me. It was almost more than I could bear after having restored relationships that were damaged prior to Mum dying, to now, having to face a different kind of grief. Or an intensified kind of grief. Layered on top of experiencing the death of my Mum, who was my last surviving parent, I had now become distanced from people who made up the very fabric of who I was. It was a complete undoing of my soul. I was already at a point of utter anguish, and when I became disconnected from these deep, nourishing sources of love and strength, I began feeling a deeper sense of loss, and the sense of stability I was trying so desperately to find was gone.

Not only did this have an immediate effect on myself, but it changed the way our other loved ones functioned. They worked to still maintain relationships while readjusting who was and wasn't mentioned in conversations and so began a delicate operation of relationships being carefully navigated within moving segments.

Over the years that followed, I wondered what had changed things for us at the time and why. I had my own protective list of 'reasons' that I could recite as if reading them from a mental scroll at the ready. I would recite these reasons with an air of hurt and righteousness. After all, I was the real victim in this saga. I was the one who laid everything on the line to care for Mum and became an avid researcher of all things to do with supporting terminal patients of sarcomatoid mesothelioma cancer. I gave everything. What more could I have done?

Hurt. Heart. Shield.

As the years went by, I found myself wavering between accepting that these once close relationships had ended and genuinely wishing them well, to slipping back into the belief that I was the victim and waiting for others to acknowledge their faults and offer an apology. Yes, I may have acted out at times, but I should be forgiven because I was under a lot of stress trying to keep my mum alive and I should be understood.

Hurt. Heart. Shield.

The anger, the hurt, the resentment, the blame. Layers of it all. Thick and dense. All layered around my heart, working to protect it from any more loss as I tried to heal its brokenness from the loss of the one who validated who I was in this world, and who loved me in a way that only she and my father could. The reality was, there was nothing anyone could have done or said that would have removed the layers of protection around my heart. I had subconsciously already decided that. The layers may have been softened, but they would have still remained as a way of protecting myself against any possible wrong move, deliberate or otherwise. I still had my heart closed to them, and I did not know how to change that.

Hurt. Heart. Shield.

Some years later, as I continued to work through the clouds of grief and confusion, I reached a place where I could look deeply into my heart, and there, I sensed a quiet and profound change within me. The path that led me here was far from smooth but instead, marked with rough patches and doubt. As I slowly opened myself up to my own uncomfortable thoughts and feelings, I began to sense a shift within. I started examining both why I felt victimised and why I was choosing to hold on to that identity which began after Mum was diagnosed. And it was by finding the courage to sit with the deeply uncomfortable feelings of vulnerability that urged me to gently uncover what was driving my own wounded reactions and responses.

I chose to hold on to the identity of the victim because I was desperately trying to create a sense of control in the uncontrollable chaos. This tactic was one I learnt to use as a child, where I would try to control a situation by emotionally and physically withdrawing. I did this with the expectation that those I felt had wronged me would be compelled to validate my wounded feelings and prove they cared about me. Prove they loved me. My deepest fear was abandonment, and I was being abandoned by the one person left who unconditionally wanted me to be happy. This triggered in me a deep, hurt response from little Stacey. By acknowledging this raw state of survival I went into after the diagnosis, I was able to connect with myself in such an honest and loving way that it brought a sweet and gentle peace that healed and broke down the layers shielding my heart. One by one, each thick layer of anger, hurt, resentment and blame eased itself away. Under these layers was a delicate, sheer layer of vulnerability. The closest layer to the heart.

When I reached this layer, I began to see my vulnerability was what connected me to myself and others. Being open to and acknowledging my own vulnerability meant I could truly see us as humans having human responses. I wasn't always aware of why I did things when I was in that raw state of survival. I made choices that were not emotionally or relationally healthy, based on wanting to protect myself, and by subconsciously reverting to a tactic I used as a child to seek love as a response to the threat of being abandoned. This deep level of honesty has no room for shame. No room for judgement about how we should have known better. No room for embarrassment. This level of honesty just is. And with it, brings the deepest knowing that within our time of grieving, we all have our own feelings, reactions, responses and truth.

Honesty. Love. Heal.

The journey of grief can be treacherous and unpredictable. We each have our own unique grief stories. Sometimes they have distanced relationships like mine, sometimes they don't at all. They are what they are, and we can hold the truth of our own unique journeys with kindness and gentleness, knowing there is no right or wrong, no shame. It just is.

Honesty. Love. Heal.

My own grief story does not end here, nor are all the loose ends tied up neatly. My story continues with an open heart to humanness and gentle steps towards vulnerability. Because close to vulnerability is love. The truth is I will always have a deep ache for us to find our way back to each other. Heart to heart, just as we are.

And through my dark journey of grief, the light at the end of the tunnel is love.

STACEY HOWES is a New Zealand-based writer who explores deep and meaningful conversations of the soul, where we truly connect as humans. Her work invites readers into the tender spaces of the heart, where healing and self-acceptance unfolds. She is a regular contributor to the Anthologia series in print and online.

BETWEEN TWO WORLDS, AGAIN

CLAUDIA CALLISTO

From a daughter of Italian immigrant parents to a widow finding her way.

I've always lived between two worlds.

Growing up as an Australian-born daughter of Italian immigrant parents, my life was shaped by two realities: the deeply traditional world of my parents and the modern, individualistic Australian world outside our front door in the western suburbs of Adelaide.

One world based on cultural traditions and unwritten rules, and the other world pulling me towards freedom and self-expression and the Australian way of life.

I was raised to play it safe. Be a *good* Italian-Australian girl.

Family was everything. You followed your family and cultural rules, you were respectful to your elders, you silently accepted things, you were humble, modest and played small, you stayed close to home, you got married, had babies, nurtured your family, you cooked and cleaned, you worked hard in a secure job and contributed financially. And just like your mother, you sacrificed your own dreams for the comfort of others.

That upbringing gave me love, connection to my culture, family and stability. It taught me resilience and how to take responsibility for my own life. But it also came with invisible walls, unspoken rules and expectations that sometimes felt like invisible chains around my neck.

People often asked what it was like growing up between two worlds.

I'd say, 'At home, I was Italian. Outside, I was Australian. But I was always the good girl. At home and outside. I was still the good girl even when I longed to make my own choices, free from the weight of tradition and unwritten cultural rules and expectations.'

I often would say it was like wearing two cultural outfits and constantly changing them, depending on where I was and who I was with.

My fellow ethnic friends and I regularly talked and laughed about the contradiction of our lives in a humorous way – the secret outings, the imposed curfews, the family expectations and guilt from wanting a different life, the endless and wonderful food at family gatherings, the exhausting cultural unwritten rules inside and outside of the home.

But underneath the laughter, we shared a heavier truth: living in two worlds meant carrying two versions of ourselves – one culture that we honoured and one that we constantly negotiated.

And yet, that in-between also gave me beautiful life gifts. I felt this great level of cultural richness in the Italian language, the cultural traditions and the deep family ties. I felt different and very knowledgeable for being trilingual, in my case navigating between Italian, French and English. I was adaptable because I had the ability to move between communities with ease and a unique identity, as I was not fully one or the other but a blend of nationalities. Finally, I had more empathy than some of my Australian-born peers as I knew the challenges my parents and our community faced being new immigrants and trying to understand and come to terms with their new reality.

I learned to *embrace the in-between*. It gave me strength. It taught me how to feel the fear and do it anyway, and extend my mindset beyond my comfort zone.

But as I reached midlife, I found myself in *another* kind of in-between – the *Sandwich Generation.* Caring for aging parents while raising my own child. Honouring the past while adapting to modern parenting practices. In addition, for me in that sandwich, there was also another layer that was *the cultural sandwich* – navigating traditional expectations from my family while living in modern Australia. *It's a strange, heavy balancing act.*

On one side, I'm raising my child in a modern Australia that is nothing like the world my parents knew. I'm trying to give him cultural Italian traditions without making them chains – teaching him to embrace his heritage, his Nonni's language, recipes and traditions that shaped me and gave me resilience. But I'm also letting him find his own way, free of the silent rules that shaped my own life.

On the other side, I'm caring for my aging parents, translating doctor's instructions, managing appointments, helping with emailing and online banking and reminding them gently that the current world has changed, even as they cling to the comfort of the old ways. Along with my sisters, I am always the 'good daughter' they raised, patient, caring, devoted and ready to help and protect their needs. They immigrated for us, their future daughters, and always worked so hard so we could have a better life than they did.

So, I'm not just sandwiched between two generations. I'm also sandwiched between two *cultures.* The traditional Italian world still whispers its expectations: *Be the caretaker. Be the dutiful daughter. Don't complain.*

The modern Australian world tells me: *Care for yourself, too. You're allowed to have time for yourself, your own well-being and travel adventures before it's too late.*

Both voices are loud. Both feel urgent and press hard against my heart.

Most days, I'm stretched thin trying to honour the past while creating a future. I juggle work requirements, my career, financial security, my own mental health, menopause, constant fatigue, my son's teenage moods and phone calls about aged-care packages. I go from workplace meetings, cultural storytelling, recording podcasts and teenage parenting to GP appointments and completing online-banking transactions for my mum. I find myself soothing my son's worries about living life without his dad by his side, his uncertain career choices as a Gen Z, while quietly hiding my own exhaustion from everyone because I don't want to burden anyone.

It's living two parallel lives on a single timeline and often in the same twenty-four hours. It is a lonely place sometimes.

The 'in-between' of the sandwich generation is invisible to many. You're carrying so much for everyone else that you forget to ask, *who's carrying me?*

Especially now that John has passed, I whisper to myself.

And yet, even there I found a new meaning.

Because in one moment, I'm passing down the same love my parents gave me. In the next, I'm rewriting what didn't serve me. I'm the bridge. The translator for the next generation. The keeper of culture *and* the quiet negotiator who softens it for the next generation.

From a young age, I did dream bigger. Much bigger than a 'good Italian girl' was expected to be. I wanted it all – travel, adventure, a career beyond the safe path, a chance to tick off my bucket-list dreams. With a mix of Italian passion and determination – some might call it stubbornness – I bent the rules my parents imposed on me and wrote new ones that I was happy with.

I felt that you could still embrace your culture without being trapped by it. You can love your family and still choose your own path.

After working hard in life and at my career and juggling between both cultural worlds as best as I could, I had to add to the mix infertility, and six years of intense IVF treatments. At the age of fifty-four, and soon after my dad's sudden passing, I left my secure career in business and accounting, and wrote my memoir *The Good Italian Girl – a personal story of awakening and redefining the cultural rules of an Australian-Italian woman.* On the day my book launched on Amazon, on 24 August 2021, it became a number one Amazon bestseller in sixteen categories in Australia, the USA and Canada.

The book led me to create a one-woman storytelling show at the Adelaide Fringe in 2022. One show only was my brave objective, but it was sold out weeks in advance. I remembered standing on stage, terrified but triumphant, reclaiming my story.

Becoming an artist and performer rather than pursuing a safe and secure career until retirement created some judgement. The Italian community thought I had lost the plot. My husband, family and friends nervously supported me despite their concerns that it might fail … but I did it anyway.

Through humour and storytelling, I created a safe space for women who were living between two worlds just like me. Together, we laughed at the struggles we grew up with, felt united as we understood each other and related to each other's similar experiences and in some ways we reclaimed our identities – not just as 'good Italian-Australian girls' but as women with choice. We felt seen, and we could still feel pride about our cultural heritage and upbringing.

And then, just two weeks after my first sold-out Adelaide Fringe show and change in career, my life shattered in an instant and a piece of me disappeared. My husband, John, died suddenly of a heart attack at his workplace.

On a Monday morning in April 2022, John woke me up and kissed me goodbye as he left for work.

'I'll call you later,' he said.

Three hours later, I stood at his workplace, hearing the words no one is ever ready for, 'He's gone.'

A sudden heart attack. No warning. No chance to say goodbye.

And just like that, I was between worlds again.

Now I live between the world I had with John and the world without him.

Grief has its own in-between. You have one foot in the world of the living, where people expect you to keep functioning, paying bills, showing up, and answering messages. One foot in the world of memory, where he still exists in every corner of my heart, so vivid it hurts.

I'm here … but I'm also there.

Grief is strange. It's the small, ridiculous things that hit the hardest. Sometimes, I cry so hard I can't breathe, and sometimes, I laugh out loud, remembering his silly jokes and the things we used to banter and tease each other about. I even miss the silly arguing over how to stack the dishwasher, leaving residue on the toothpaste tube and how to cook with more salt in the pasta sauce.

Sometimes I still reach for my phone to tell him something … then I remember that he is not contactable anymore and I can only stare at his picture on my mobile wallpaper.

When you lose someone you've loved for over thirty-five years, the world goes dim. There's a hollow quiet that echoes at night. John was my safe place, my soft landing, my partner in love, life and laughter.

He saw beauty in ordinary things. Maybe that's why he was such a gifted photographer. Through his lens, he didn't just take photos, he captured souls. Now, I hold onto those images to remember the life and love we shared – a memory no one can steal.

The *before* was full with family, friends, culture, connections and adventures. I was fortunate to be truly known and loved by someone special. The *after* is a quiet house, an empty bed, solo parenting, a small circle of loyal family and friends and an ache so deep, it feels like it is never going to end, and a silence so loud it almost has a sound.

Sometimes, people don't know what to say. They tilt their heads and gently ask, *'How are you?'*

And I just smile and say, *'I am doing OK, thank you for asking.'*

But inside I whisper, *'I'm between worlds.'*

I feel like I am not living here without him. I'm just … learning. Learning to live with the ache. Learning to carry him in my heart instead of beside me. Learning to confidently make life decisions without him. Learning to be my true self. Learning to be a solo parent and to be both parents to Marcus our son. Learning to let go of the people who abandoned me and who no longer call or care anymore.

I think of the old Italian widows I grew up around – women who wore black for years after their husbands died, who still cooked their husbands' favourite meals as if they might walk through the door. I used to think, *'How sad. They've never moved on.'*

It is a part of the Italian culture I never really understood. The wearing of full black until they passed away themselves. The quiet life they lead in their homes, curtains drawn, mourning in the dark, never drawing attention to themselves and playing small within the community. They are labelled 'Vedova', a term describing widow Italian women.

Now, I understand.

They weren't stuck. They were living *with* their love. Carrying it forward. Living between worlds and following their cultural expectations.

But I have chosen a different path. I refuse to let grief chain me the way tradition once tried to. Losing John has made me even more determined to live fully, for both of us.

Time is never guaranteed. John wasn't ready to go – we had so many dreams still waiting. So now I dream them for both of us.

I say John's name because he is still my person and his heart and dreams now live inside me. I believe that by saying his name every day, I am whispering that he made a difference within our lives and that he mattered.

I miss his hugs so much, the ones where I could physically and emotionally lean into him. I always felt protected and heard, even if I was complaining. What I would trade for another minute of those hugs and the feeling of love and safety.

Even in this in-between – between love and loss, between the past and present – I can still feel him. I can still hear him. Maybe that's enough to keep me going for a while

I still hear John's voice, *'Come on, bubbee. Get up. Be brave. You can do anything you set your mind to and keep going after your dreams.'*

Even now, I still talk to John, especially when I am visiting his grave each week. I tell him about Marcus, about our son's teenage moods and about the little victories in my day. Sometimes, I even ask for a sign. Anything I request, a feather, a bird, a butterfly or if you really want to help, tell me the lotto numbers in my dreams.

Grief changes your lens. It shows you who truly stands with you.

And sometimes I sit at his grave in complete disbelief at how some family have abandoned me soon after his death, placing distance between us. Leaving silence where there should have been comfort. It has hurt deeply – especially after thirty-five years together – and confused our son Marcus. Deep down, I know if the roles were reversed and I passed away first, my family would never have done that to him and our child. I am grateful that my own family, my son and close friends have become my lifeline and biggest supporters.

My Italian upbringing taught me about family, resilience, and the power of community. But it also taught me how deeply we feel loss. Because when someone dies, it's not just *one person* who goes – it's a whole lifetime of shared meals, moments and memories. Unfortunately, I feel my Italian culture does not know how to deal with grief very well. I see an example of this when the deceased person's name is rarely mentioned after a short time.

So now I'm the one left to carry those worlds and to keep John's name alive in future conversation. To keep his legacy alive.

Just like I learned to embrace being between Italian and Australian, I'm learning – slowly – to live between love and loss.

Because love doesn't vanish when someone is gone. It shifts. It becomes memory. It becomes strength. It becomes the whisper that tells you to keep going.

Because grief is just love with nowhere to go.

And my love for John … it still has a million places to go. Into my stories. My laughter. My work. My community.

Even in this grief – *this new in-between* – I know storytelling will help me heal my heart.

Being a creative artist together with the support of my son Marcus, my mum Luisa, my sisters Laura, Diana, Celeste, my friends and the women within my community, I will keep going and create a braver and more adventurous life and become the best version of myself.

So, after a year of mourning and endless tears, I decided to return to performing at the Adelaide Fringe and creating new cultural events for my women's community, expanding my storytelling through creating a podcast called *The Good Italian Girl and Friends*. I also balanced creativity with the stability of employed work to keep myself and my son financially safe.

Despite feeling some initial judgement from some family and my Italian community for returning to performing on stage only a year after John's passing, rather than wearing black, playing small and remaining hidden at home behind closed curtains for the rest of my life, I was determined to keep telling our story – mine and John's – just like I told the story of my parents and my culture. I'll talk about the funny bits, the annoying bits, and the beautiful, ordinary, everyday love we shared.

Because honouring John is not only about keeping his name alive. It's about showing that even in *love and loss*, we can still find meaning, connection and courage.

Love doesn't end when someone is gone. We are still together, and he is still here, guiding me.

In the end, my Australian-Italian culture played a huge role in initially shaping me into the adult I became … but grief has reshaped me into the person I will be in the future. Culture taught me about family, but grief taught me about love and courage.

I am still between two worlds. But now I know how to live there.

P.S.

Dear Claudia,

Please be kinder to yourself as you have never lived this life before, and every single day you are walking into new territory. You don't need to have it all figured out and to have all the answers. No one is expecting you to. Give yourself some grace, because you are showing up every day and doing your best, and your best is good enough.

It is OK to disappoint other people as long as you don't end up disappointing yourself. If you're living within your alignment and living within your expectations, you should not worry about their expectations of you.

It is OK to show up and be seen exactly as you are. You have gifts within you that your community needs. You have a light that shines. When you allow yourself to be in the fullness of those gifts and light, not only do you help other people, you also help heal yourself and be in alignment with who you are. The true gift is being exactly who you are. You are everything you always have been looking for.

Allow the new version of you to bloom, do not hold yourself back. You already have what you need inside you. You have all the skills, wisdom and resources that you can draw on for this next chapter and to build your future.

I love you, and I am incredibly proud of you.

Love, Claudia

CLAUDIA CALLISTO is an Italian-Australian Cultural Storyteller, Best Selling Author of *The Good Italian Girl*, Performing Fringe Artist, Podcast Creator and Host of The Good Italian Girl and Friends, Speaker and Co-founder of Shining Light. Claudia's work celebrates heritage, connects generations and champions the voices of Italian-Australian women, honouring the past, embracing the present, and inspiring the future.

@claudiacallisto | shininglightcd.com.au

DARKNESS TO REBIRTHING

NATARSHA WILSON

Dedicated to the strongest person I know, Nicole.

This chapter is about being pulled into darkness. Consumed and unable to keep my head above the water, even though I knew how to swim. In my mind, it felt like I was on a carousel while trying to strengthen myself to hop off once the ride stopped. It never did. How is it even possible, with hormones circulating through me and the voices in my head, to define who I am, what I believe, and what society expects of me? How can I get off the carousel?

My favourite saying is 'I'm not a victim, I'm not a survivor, I'm a warrior.' When I'm called a victim, I feel attached to the darkness and negativity I've experienced. It places me in the exact spot I need to escape, still sitting on the horse going around that carousel, but wanting off. When I'm called a survivor, I keep trying to get off the carousel while it's slowly spinning. I have only started to rebirth myself, with the darkness still holding onto me, even if it is with one finger, and somehow it still holds a connection and allows the past to define who I am. Those words are not how I want to be described. *I'm a warrior.* It's both survivor and victim together – as one. To me, the word warrior feels like I have disconnected from the darkness; dissociated from those feelings and thoughts that held me down. I gained the strength to push the red button on the carousel to enable it to stop.

The darkness began during my high school years. I had negative thoughts in my head, was unable to focus academically, and felt like I didn't fit in because I didn't have a boyfriend. I didn't wear what the celebrities did, and I didn't have an up-to-date phone. Going around in circles, I wondered what people thought if I wasn't allowed to attend the party? Or going to the party alone? Being a teenager was hard; trying to fit in was harder. The dark fog grabbed a hold of me, slowly clenching its claws in.

Never single. I always needed to be in a relationship. Was I finding relationships for comfort? Did the relationships happen because everyone else had boyfriends? Was I being social because I was scared of being alone? Did I even love myself enough to allow someone to love me? How amazing it would be if future me could have advised now me that it will be OK. Comparing myself to how the movies, television shows and magazines played out enhanced the darkness; it was what fed it.

The Darkness gripped onto me as the carousel spun faster and faster. I didn't know if it would ever slow down. How could I know who I truly was if I was never alone? While I looked out to the world, sitting on that horse, spinning, the world was all blurry. As I sat there alone, it still wasn't slowing down because I wasn't allowing myself to grow independently. With my pain and an abnormal bleed, I was scared of reality and to get assistance because I worried what others would think if I complained. These are the reasons I could not grow.

Do I want answers? Why is this feeling of dissociation taking over? Why won't the ride stop? As I became dizzy, my eyes closed. I needed to find the source of the light. I needed to get off. I wanted to be reborn.

Living in the darkness was cold, numbing, and I withdrew from the world and my body. But I saw a glimmer of hope. I dismounted one leg at a time. I held on to the rails. I shook from fear of rejection, reactions, of being different to what I only knew.

I attended appointments, allowed myself to open and even considered that I'm not like everyone else. I need to build my own path to find the answers to push forward. Accepting help and a diagnosis gave me the freedom to move more freely around life because I accepted myself.

Take a breath; you got this. Stop chasing the movie life; this is real, this is your moment, this is your time to shine, without relying on anyone else. Once you are happy alone, you can be that positive energy to raise happiness in others. Self-dating, escaping to the beach, a bath with a home-cooked meal just for me, enough leftovers for the next day, and enjoying my own company. I have done it; I have learnt what brings me happiness.

I know how to be reborn, have self-worth, get guidance from loved ones, and disable the thoughts of judging and comparing myself to others. Once I started to slip into comfort and began to notice that the darkness was trying to catch up to me, everything slowed down. I escaped it, even if it's just one small change; the change is what alters the direction.

I'm going to make that appointment to find the answers that keep me up at night. Spoil myself with a date-night alone. Binge-watch my favourite movie. Because I am a warrior. I'm no longer that victim on the carousel, spinning really fast. I'm no longer the survivor who is still on the carousel, even though it is turning slowly. I'm the warrior who pushed the red STOP button and got off, facing the darkness head-on, allowing myself to feel positively uncomfortable, which allowed me to have a rebirthing, giving me a new outlook on the world without expectations. From the darkness to rebirthing, now let's celebrate being a woman.

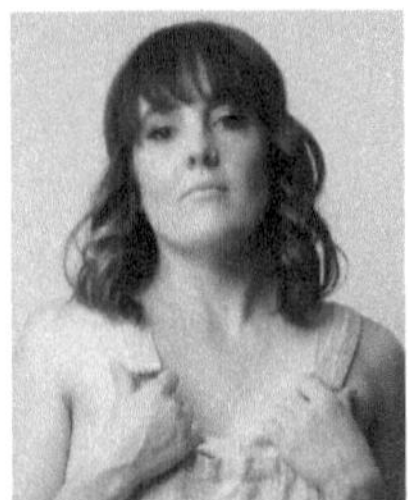

NATARSHA WILSON is a Nurse in women's health, sexologist, menopause coach and podcast co-host.

FIRE WE KEEP

CHRISTIE-LEE DIDOVICH

Dedicated to all the little girls whose fires were extinguished.
May we reclaim the embers that burn within.

I've always carried the scent of rebellion. It was stitched into me like an invisible thread tying me to a lineage of chaos. From my earliest memories, I was the child who strayed too far from the path, the one with a bloody nose and keen eyes, the one who chased the danger. Trouble didn't find me. I hunted it down.

Breaking rules was like breaking bread. It was a ritual, it came easy, it was therapeutic. I climbed too high, ran too fast, dared to the edge of boundaries that other children never dreamed of approaching. Trouble became a kind of initiation. Every scraped elbow, every cranky adult, every sideways glance felt like confirmation that I was made of something different.

And isn't that what every child secretly craves? To know they are different, to feel that there is something extraordinary in their veins? For me, rebellion was that confirmation. It told me, *you will never live an ordinary life.* I knew I was not given a life of ease. It showed me a life not domesticated, but free-range, away from the path others so heavily desire. Illumination to a different way of being. That was my truth. I would never be small. That's for sure.

Sometimes I wonder though, was it destiny? Was this script carved into my bones before I even took my first breath? Or did the countless moments of defiance I collected write me into this way of being? Was the inheritance I bear one of chaos, or was I simply the author of my own wild story? Perhaps it was both. Perhaps we were handed a compass and told nothing about the map. Dropped off in the desert of life, forced to find my own way back amidst the projections of the world around me.

I imagine the women before me, the ancestors I've never met, must have carried this same fire. The women who laughed too loud, loved too bold and those who slipped through the cracks of a polite and polished society. The women who could not be contained, who therefore became the topic of town whispers. I feel them in me, perhaps disobedient grandmothers or uncontrollable aunts. Their defiance is in my core. Their unapologetic yeses beat in my chest. Something I have no tangible evidence of in this realm, but I know to be the truth that runs in my veins. An otherworldly knowing that I simply cannot explain.

Even in my infancy, bending my strong will was an unmatched task. I had a catchphrase before I even understood most words in our language: can't want to. Those three words became my blueprint. I was not here to bow down. I was not here to perform for approval. I was powerful. I was strong-willed. I was going to get what I wanted. However that came about. I didn't know yet what freedom truly meant, but my body knew. The story had already been written. The world dressed as a polite prison held no merit in my young mind.

The people who shaped my world were explorers. They chased meaning through music, art, politics and through the questions others never dared to bring to life. Curiosity was simply dinner-table conversations. I absorbed the lens they wore. I learnt that if a stop sign appears, tap it, test it, check if it is real. If it is real, learn to climb it. If it is not, walk through, walk around, discover what it's made of, question every part of its existence until you understand.

And as a child desperate for safety and belonging, it was disorienting. On one hand, it held pride, yet the other revealed the truth of the world we live in. The outside world was not safe to be me. I learnt early the repercussions this rebellion imprisoned me with. To live as the child of disruption was to always stand on a threshold, parts begging for acceptance, others yearning to be myself, yet never fully at home. It taught me to read rooms like literature, to sense the subtle shifts in the air only available to those who know rejection in their bones. I learnt to track behaviours, small eye movements and tensing when I speak a little too loud. I learned the art of shrinking. I compressed my truth. I learned the dance of silence. I believed my words equalled danger. I knew fitting in lit the hearth of safety, no matter the cost of the wood. Individuality was not celebrated. It was cursed and shunned away. To question was to sin. To resist was to risk exile. The curriculum hid their agenda in plain sight, 'be small, be good, be easy.'

But wildness never dies. It only goes underground.

The flames within smothered, but the embers remained. I waited for oxygen. The problem child. The girl would excel if she only applied herself. They didn't understand that I *was* applying myself. I was studying freedom. Majoring in the pushback. Minoring in confrontation. Deciphering the cage with every corner of my skin. Rules were suffocating. Even when framed as protection, they pressed like a weight on my chest. I wanted to be good. I truly did. It asked for obedience in exchange for belonging. It asked for silence in exchange for safety. And so, rebellion the highest point in Maslow's pyramid. Not because I loved the chaos, more so my soul required it.

Two worlds defined my growing years. One gave me space of expression through clothes, through music, through small acts of defiance that allowed me to breathe. The other demanded obedience. It begged I be the good girl. One offered the safety of expression, move your body, wear your truth, sing as if the banshee entered your lungs. The other offered the safety of growth in reality. The tension of that double life shaped me. My clothes became my craft. My music became my canvas. If I couldn't scream, I let my outfit do it for me. A walking billboard explaining what was on the inside. I learned how an outfit could be a symbol, how a song could be a spell, how my thick eyeliner could be an anchor to the place my soul refused to abandon.

Authority didn't take kindly to my fire. My spirit refused to bow. I started to understand something liberating.

1. Approval and belonging are not the same thing.
2. That chasing the first often costs you the second.

And so, I walked a tightrope. Too much to be ignored, too defiant to be accepted. To exist in that realm meant learning the loneliness of the rebel heart.

Adulthood presented an unfamiliar twist. Saying yes when I wanted to say no became my downfall. I traded tiny pieces of myself for a place at tables that offered me crumbs and called it a meal. At first, the yeses seemed harmless, but each one that betrayed my own truth carved another notch out of my spirit. Being uncomfortable became the tax I paid for belonging. To earn connection, I learned to silence myself. To be loved, I shrunk. I became the person who anticipated needs before they were named, who apologised without reason, who turned down the volume on every device so the speakers of the world rung loudest. The unravelling hit me hard. Burnout. Bullying. Heartbreak. Each collapse stripped away another false layer until nothing was left but fragments.

Then a realisation emerged. From those ashes, something unexpected bloomed. The parts of me I thought were broken were seeds. The cracks in my foundation became fruitful soil. Day by day, the wildness I had buried sprouting a new form. This time, not destructive but creative. Not reckless but powerful. I learned the difference between burning it all down and lighting the way.

The woman who emerged was not brand new. She was the girl I had always been. I had reclaimed her. She had always been there, waiting, holding her breath beneath the polite layers. That final exhale, giving her permission to exist exactly how originally intended.

My voice grew louder, to lead. My body became something I admired. My presence began to shine. I found a village of laughter, love and connection. A circle that welcomed me without condition, where truth was not a liability, but a language embraced by all. I learned to listen to myself like a sacred text.

Now I see rebellion for what it truly is. Leadership in disguise. It is the willingness to be first through the door and the first to take the questions. The one who has to hold the despair and joy in one hand. It is the audacity to ask and show where you can be different and still be accepted, and then amongst the chaos, cultivate the strength to hold yourself in place when people laugh or walk away. It is the known certainty that your inner compass is pointing north, no matter how stormy the seas around you get. It is the kind of leadership that is not taught in schools, not handed down in manuals, not rewarded with medals or certificates. It is forged in fire, in silence, in the spaces where you are forced to reckon with yourself and decide whether you will bend or break.

My rebellion is now more than just my own. It's a tool to lead others toward the resistance. To show them how to embody the veracity of self. I began to weave my rebellion into something great.

A vehicle for leadership, for creation, for transformation. Every boundary I set, every time I said no to what did not align and yes to what fuelled me, and every time I chose myself, it became a brick in the foundation of my own authority. The more I honoured my own rules, the more magnetic my life became.

This rebellion became the beacon for others to follow. The ones who have fallen into the void of silence and suppression. I began to mentor, to lead, to create spaces where women could claim their own truth without apology. Creating these places showed me that my trials and tribulations were more than just my own. It was the blueprint for others to reclaim their own fire. Because every collapse, every burnout, every heartbreak had carved out the route I now walk with confidence. This map is the reason I now finally understand the full circle my lineage gifted me. The ancestors whose fire I carry, the mentors who taught me to question everything, the ones who stitched the tapestry I wear. I am both beacon and pilgrim. I walk in the shadows so I can create the light. I now walk into rooms with the knowledge that my voice matters, that my fire matters, that my rebellion matters. Not because I am loud, not because I demand attention, but because I have been forged to hold my own space. I have been tested. I have burned. I have rebuilt.

The rebellion is no longer my symptom. It is my language, my playbook, my gift. It tells the story of resilience, of courage, of transformation. The fire within me is no longer hidden. It rises, it spreads, it illuminates. It calls to other wild souls, the ones who have been crumbling under the weight of expectation, the ones whose yeses have been stolen, the ones whose voices have been silenced.

This rebellion, this fire, is not just mine. It is ours. It is the inheritance of the women before me, before us all, and it is the gift to all the women who will come after us. And with this, I have found not only freedom, but purpose, power and a home within myself that no one can ever take away.

CHRISTIE-LEE DIDOVICH is a writer, coach and boundary-breaker with over thirteen years of experience helping women reclaim their power and build lives that feel like their own. Having walked through anxiety, depression, substance abuse, a narcissistic relationship and grief, Christie-Lee doesn't just write about healing, she's done the work. She is well known for empowering women to speak up and stop performing for approval. As an author, she brings that same clarity and conviction to the page. Christie-Lee has a weekly podcast called Your Boundary Bestie with digestible episodes to guide women toward a life they love. Available on Spotify and Apple Podcasts every Wednesday morning at 7am.

@christieleedidovich

SEEDS OF SISTERHOOD

EMMA RIGNEY

Dedicated to my Garden Sisters, who held my hand and walked with me down the path towards healing.

I sat staring at my phone, with the information about The Garden filling my screen. A cyclic sanctuary created and hosted by cycle mentor and educator Daniella Elias. She'd created a year-long container focused on honouring our inner ecosystems, holding space to rediscover our womanhood, learning to honour our needs, and to journey with her on a path of self-exploration. So, why was I hesitating at the possibility of joining a circle offering exactly what I so desperately craved? Because this space would be shared with other women.

For a time, I'd felt like my connection to self had slowly disappeared. My life was happy – I had a safe home full of love and support, and endless pupper cuddles. I had freedom to explore creative ventures. I had time to spend with family and friends, and I was relishing being witness to our niblings growing up. But I felt unsettled within myself. I could feel my body going through the physical changes that come with age (hello, perimenopause). I was struggling through energy spikes and slumps I didn't know how to manage. I felt lost in my physical body and even more lost as I struggled emotionally and mentally to cope. It was uncomfortable to admit to myself that I'd lost my way. It was even more uncomfortable to admit it to anyone else.

After much hesitation and deliberation, I committed myself to joining the space. I wanted information, and Daniella had it. The structure of The Garden and the detailed curriculum within was everything my body and soul were craving. My plan going in was simple – move through the monthly Zoom sessions and educate myself about my cycle, the changes currently presenting themselves and how to make the best of this new normal. I did not anticipate that I would connect with the other women in the container.

Although I felt anxious about group participation, I wanted to fully commit to the process, which meant a round of introductions on our first session together. My heart beat rapidly in my chest. Perspiration gathered on my skin. My ears were ringing, and my mouth and throat were dry, even after a desperate chug of water. I was listening as the other Garden Keepers introduced themselves, knowing my turn was imminent.

Suddenly, all eyes were on me. With a huge breath that didn't feel like it came close to reaching my lungs, I unmuted my microphone and tried to speak. But no words came out. Instead, fear and nerves overwhelmed me, and tears spilled forth. I grappled with my words. Eventually, I sputtered out my name and stammered through some of the reasons I'd joined The Garden. I heard the shame in my voice as I apologised for the tears, and I quickly hit mute again while I attempted to gather myself.

Once the Zoom call ended, I felt completely overwhelmed to the point my body shut down. I cried myself to sleep. The next day, I saw a number of new messages waiting for me in The Garden group chat on Instagram. I opened and read the messages, and I found myself in tears all over again. But this time it was for a whole different reason. Part of it was surprise, but mostly because the words that greeted me were so unexpected. I was called brave for pushing through and speaking. I was told they were grateful I'd shared. I was reminded this was a safe space and I could share as much or as little as I wanted. I felt held. I felt heard, seen and understood.

This support was the opposite of the trauma I'd experienced in my past at the hands of other women. No one made fun of me for expressing my emotions or my anxiety. No one joked or made snide, passive-aggressive remarks about me or about anything I'd said. I wasn't equipped to handle feeling so supported, and especially not so immediately. Of course, the fear filtered through in a matter of seconds. Was this a trap, with the insults and 'negging' and betrayals of trust to follow later? This is what I'd experienced so often in the past. Was this what was in store for me again? These questions would soon be answered because, unbeknown to me, the seeds of sisterhood had been planted.

~

My hesitation in The Garden, given its group structure, comes from trauma. The sister wounds I carry began in my teens and have continued throughout my adult life. These wounds have left me somewhat untrusting and doubtful of women in general – especially groups of women.

I've always felt somewhat out of step with the women around me. A lot of it circles back to my choices and how, without exactly meaning to, I go against the grain. From simple things like my sense of style and hobbies, to bigger things like my beliefs, my career endeavours, or choosing not to have children. Time after time, I begin to trust again, to believe I've found trust and safety. And time after time, I am wounded. Sometimes it's subtle, most times it is not.

I try not to dwell, but being hurt repeatedly at the hands of other women is wearing. All the choices I've made have shaped the life I so dearly love. But they also, at times, deepened the sense of distance between me and other women. Not always, but often enough to leave an impression. And those little impressions … they add up. It makes for an isolating experience, one where the possibility of a new friendship is met with doubt, hesitation and fear. Will I once again share an experience, or trauma, or personal insight about myself in what I believe to be a safe space only to have this shared or used against me later? Will I be ostracised? Teased? Will this be the woman who finally goes too far and breaks me?

I'm never certain if it's me or them. It's most likely a combination. I do not desire or endeavour to live my life to please anyone else. And I understand that I am not for everyone. Nor do I want to be. But it can be a lonely way to experience life. I see myself as resilient, and I remain optimistic, loyal, loving and very much myself. I am a unique individual and, despite some of the things I've endured throughout my life, I remain true to my own heart.

I try to remind myself that, of course, not every woman I encounter will wound me. I have been included as much as I have been excluded. Supported as much as I have been torn down. Loved as much as I have been hated. But the ones who have hurt me have left marks so deep, I did not believe they could ever be healed. They left me with trust issues, with a fear of sharing who I really am. I never feel completely safe with those outside my innermost circle. And being constantly dragged down wears on you, and it had left me feeling closed off to the possibility of making new friends in my forties.

~

After only two months in The Garden, I realised something felt different. I was forming a connection with the six women with whom I was sharing this space. Not an ordinary connection, but something genuine and deeply authentic. What began as a shared desire to better understand ourselves gradually became a safe, grounding space where we could show up exactly as we were and speak whatever needed to be spoken.

I felt the shift within. Slow at first, but unmistakable. My walls began to come down. I still guarded myself, but I could feel the protective casing I'd built around my heart being chipped away. Together, we laughed, we cried, we celebrated our wins and shared our disappointments. We moved through all the cyclical wisdom Daniella had for us, sharing our personal insights and stories along the way. We held space for each other as it was needed and listened with open hearts. I found myself not only trusting these women but craving their company.

I cannot remember how the idea of meeting in real life was born. I carried lingering fears – being together online is an entirely different experience to sharing a physical space. But we did all agree it was a must. Daniella created a sacred space for us, and in the last weekend of June, we gathered.

The anxiety I felt was literally sickening. My past trauma came back, front and centre. Groups of women were always my worst tormentors. Was it about to happen all over again? I tried desperately not to overthink it, but all the hesitation and doubt I'd felt upon joining The Garden returned, and I began to fear that maybe I'd made a mistake. As it turned out, those fears, though valid, had no place here. We greeted each other with open arms and open hearts. It was like the oldest of friends coming together. There was no awkwardness or discomfort. The weekend was filled with surprise gifts, hearty home-cooked meals, quiet moments of reflection, deep conversations and comfortable silence. Not once did I feel the need to retreat to my own room. Not once did I feel overwhelmed. Not once did I feel anything other than safe. The only tears I cried were ones of happiness and release.

At the close of our gathering, Daniella asked us all to say one word that summed up how the weekend left us feeling. My mind first turned to all the negative things I'd experienced in the past, but these memories were quickly replaced with the joy, love, connection and authenticity I'd experienced in the past two days. And before I'd even fully considered it, one word tumbled out of my mouth.

Healed.

My year in The Garden, and our subsequent in-person gathering, taught me so much about myself. I reconnected with my body and my soul, and became comfortable in my own skin again. I had a place I could be fully present, fully loved and fully myself. A place I could embrace all my quirks and no longer needed to apologise for just being me. I no longer felt tethered to my past trauma. I no longer felt defined by it. It did not belong to me anymore.

Sisterhood is about being surrounded by women who allow you to be who you are. Authentically and genuinely you, without apology. All your quirks, your flaws, your low moments are embraced as fully as your kindness, loyalty and every other quality you bring.

When we are surrounded by the right women, we are empowered to go forth in all our glory.

When you find one sister, it is a beautiful thing. She will lift you higher, love you with all that she has, embrace you in your sorrow and guide you with her light when you see only darkness. But when you find more than one sister, that is your tribe. Your sisterhood. It is a blessing to have multiple sisters. Every one brings something into your life that you don't even realise you were missing. Each woman will contribute a little of themselves to you, and when all these pieces fit together, your heart will be whole.

They will leave you healed.

EMMA RIGNEY is a content creator, author, and ceramic artist. She is the founder of Shutter and Scribe Creative, where she creates authentic UGC videos and long-form copy to help brands reach their people. Emma also creates hand-built pottery in her studio (Emma Does Pottery), writes short stories, and is currently writing her debut novel. She loves dabbling in all things creative! When she's not behind the lens or keyboard, you'll find Emma tending her garden, walking her dog Neo, practising yoga or lost in a Dean Koontz thriller.

LOST

NATALIE SIMES

To my true and beautiful daughter, Macy. Always trust your heart, especially when you are the only one to hear its call. And to my sisters, both born and chosen. You are not lost. I see you. And I love you.

They sit in a circle, facing each other, yet afraid to look up. Hesitancy fills the air. They slowly raise their eyes, desperately hoping to be seen, and willing themselves not to run from the room. There is fear here too – but stronger than fear, there is trust, and love. Light and shade. The contrast. They know they can't hide any longer. They are lost girls functioning as grown women desperately wanting to be found. The cloaks of identity weigh heavy. On their bodies. On their souls. And it is time. They feel it with every inch of their being. They make a silent pledge: I will no longer abandon my soul to honour my identity. I am here. In this body, at this time, in this life. One chance. I am alive.

Identity: Who we choose to be in this world to feel safe. And often more than that, who we believe we need to be to belong. Or the contrast; yet still identity. Who we choose to be to prove to the world that we don't belong. It's more than the roles we play. It's a cloak we choose to wear. Usually many cloaks. The good girl. The rock. The smart one. The workaholic. The rebel. The positive one. The martyr. The black sheep. The list is exhaustive. And perhaps the most challenging of all – the chameleon. Always becoming exactly who you perceive others need you to be.

We collect many identities along the way as we traverse life. Often starting in childhood as we learn our place in our families and then gathered as we make our way in the world.

The cloaks allow us to hide. They're protective. Our armour. Often comforting. But sometimes heavy. Burdensome. Suffocating. We take them off and often slip another straight back on. The exposure and vulnerability of being uncloaked, naked and revealed, being too much to take.

But we continue to name ourselves in ways that are too small for our souls and, eventually, we feel lost, never really knowing why we often feel untethered. Why there is a constant feeling of being unsettled. Is this what we are here for? We bury those feelings. Because our lives are good. We're happy. But still, the feelings remain.

How to be true to who we are? To share all of who we are and what we see without fear? To believe that others might want to truly know us and trust in us. To allow others to know more than just an idea of us. Why would they trust? When we don't trust ourselves. When we so often believe that we must show up in a certain way in this life to receive love. To be accepted.

And even those who dare venture past our layered protection are often kept slightly out of reach. Internally, we're begging them to see us, but we won't surrender; we cling to the comfort of our cloaks. We pull them tighter around us. Until we are lost beneath them.

The loneliness becomes palpable. And we're tired. So very tired. Our soul chooses us, knowing the potential of the heights we can soar and the depths we can reach.

Yet we choose our identities over and over and deny our knowing, deny our truth and our heart.

The good girl often becomes the adult who doesn't trust her instincts. She analyses every move, she doesn't take risks, she fits perfectly in her box and never makes waves. She is reminded that what she can contribute to the world will be her making. She's often loved by all, respected, loyal. She controls all the moves because she always thinks before she speaks and acts. And she's safe. And she believes that's important. She strives for unattainable perfection. She will bend over backwards. Even when it breaks her. Her calm outside is in contrast to her screaming insides. And it's inevitable that the pain of being the good girl will be too much to bear, and her insides overflow to her outsides.

Often when you wander through life seeking safety, cloaking yourself in identities that don't quite fit, armoured up, very few possibilities present themselves. Everything seems too hard, and the chances that do appear seem too risky. Life is steady, predictable, and you are fully in control. Exhale. But you can't exhale. Living life in perceived safety is like holding your breath forever. Painful, contracted, death-ing. Because inevitably, you will attract what you believe.

The good girl will always attract situations that ask her to abandon herself.

The layers of fear run deep. And you often wonder if you can penetrate the depths that they hold in your body. The impossible peeling back of the layers, one by one. The layers cling. They wrap themselves right back on to make you question if your right to breathe freely is something you will ever attain.

It's time to remove the cloaks. To trust. Exhale.

And there is relief.

She knocks on the door. Quietly at first, and then more insistent. I know who she is. A much-needed friend; but I answer the door as though she's a stranger. Comfort floods the house as she crosses the threshold. Like all the lights have been turned on at once. But she startles me. I turn her away. Her light too bright for my tired eyes. And I'm back in the darkness. Rejecting the invitation to feel into my heart. Intuition. How to embrace and trust her? Her knowing doesn't fit with the identity I've so carefully crafted. But she's always been knocking. And she won't go away.

Sometimes the most vulnerable thing we can do is to stop being who we perceive everyone else needs us to be, and start being who we need us to be. To drop the identities we have cast upon ourselves. To listen. To acknowledge that we're tired of squeezing ourselves into coats that no longer fit; or maybe never fit. Or perhaps they are cloaks of comfort. There when we need them but easily taken off – like your favourite jacket; there to keep you warm when you step into the cold. The wrapping around feels truly protective. Comforting. Like a warm hug. Are these cloaks of identity? Or are they what we choose to put on when our intuition reveals we need protection? Or comfort? Or warmth? Put on, but re-hooked when no longer needed.

Maybe our soul is showing us that life is a wild dance of becoming and unbecoming. That when we see and acknowledge our identities, there is an invitation to take off what is no longer ours to carry.

What does life look like when you allow your perceived 'weird' self to be your public self? To introduce yourself, not only to the world, but to yourself, perhaps for the first time.

What does it feel like to truly know yourself? To reveal your whole self.

We've all had moments where we fully shed the cloaks, and it's liberating. But then regret. And fear. Protection at all costs.

We're often taught from birth to stay quiet, to be small, to fit ourselves into a perfectly constructed puzzle, squeezed into a certain shape, stuck, perfect. Uncomfortably perfect. Or we rebel, and chaos reigns.

Why are we so afraid of ourselves? We limit. We control. We sacrifice. We reject self and armour up. We seek perceived safety.

But what if we indulge? Even overindulge? What if we indulge in our humanity? Indulge in our passions. Indulge in our emotions. Reject perfection. Trust our instincts. Speak up.

What if we remember that true self is love? What if we over-indulge in love?

What if we celebrate the fullness of each other? If we leave nothing left unsaid. If we show ourselves fully to the world, knowing it's no-one's fault that we're hiding. That those before us wished they could be free, but never believed it possible.

True power is admitting the truth of who you are. Right now, I am an almost empty outline. A smattering of distinct markings, but mostly coloured with chalk – easily washed away for the next person to colour me how they need me to be. And I allow it. I choose it. Too afraid to stand out. Too afraid to operate in full colour, for fear of not belonging to my family. We are all silent to the people we truly are – all too afraid to be anything other than grey. Colour is seen as an attack. And it's often red. And the red is anger. There for a moment but quickly buried back beneath the grey. Colour is what we all crave – some more ready than others. I must be the colour of love and mark us all with her generosity.

Why not risk yourself from a place of genuine self-love? Be a house full of you. Allow your feelings and knowing to cascade and lead to something truer and more beautiful. For there is no peace in hiding. Pain is in the resistance of who you know yourself to be.

Do not allow yourself to be named, or name yourself, in ways that are too small for you. Or name others in ways that are too small for them. That is not our job. That is not our right. We are not meant to be fully put together – for the cracks are doorways for us to walk through. To explore. To discover. To live. We are the sum of all our individual parts. And we don't need to hide.

I've spent most, if not all my life, speaking what I believe others want to hear from me. Or staying silent. Turning away from myself so I fit in, so I belong. I am controlled. I am measured. Only showing that of myself I perceive others want to receive. Or control becomes too much. And I hurt those I love. And it's all steeped in disconnection. In an effort to be who I believe people want me to be, I've disconnected from myself, from my voice. I'm stuck on mute for all the things I want to say, to speak my heart. There has been a peeling off, an openness, a trusting in myself. And it's led to deep connection. To truth. To honesty. To deep love.

Relationships are about committing to loving each version of another, as their layers come off and we all remember who we truly are. Often in our closest relationships, we cloak each other. We come in with our identities, both inherited and taught and chosen, and instinctively drape those cloaks over those we love. We want to protect them. But often they feel trapped. Capped. And we're completely unaware. Control masked as love. But it feels like we are showing love. That is the intent. But it's not the result. And resentment enters. And the identities we wear and share become less protective, and more stifling. Resistance. Regret. Pain. Anger. Illness.

There is sadness here. Sadness for the pain of making others feel small. And suffocated. For the pain we cause each other. But there is also love here. And a commitment to seeing; to staying present and to being committed to uncloaking each other.

We cling so tightly to our identities for safety, when the truth is, when we allow ourselves to be in our full, unfiltered self around those we love, those we trust, it gives permission for them to do the same. We begin to feel truly safe to be in our full expression. We don't hold back. We begin to see and feel we are loved here. Accepted.

Celebrated for our humanity. There is no room for perfection in our closest relationships. Simply a beautiful dance between souls who acknowledge and appreciate each other's flawed humanity. Who love no matter what. This is the truest version of life to be lived. Sometimes heartbreaking. But always beautiful. True safety. Honesty.

Life experiences will have you see and open your eyes to a big, beautiful world that many others will come to know because of you. The truth is that life will deliver moments that will break your heart, and you realise that these identities you've clung to so tightly are not worth the pain of an unlived life. That you have never really been lost. That you were always right below the surface. And trusting that your people will find you; and they do. They see you. And they love you. You will see you can unravel quickly. You won't be a picture of perfection. You will be supported. No longer lost girls functioning as grown women. But grown women trusting themselves fully. Leading the way for their children, for future generations, who will always find their way home.

Maybe the most vulnerable thing we can do is to be committed to the road to discovering or uncovering who you truly are. Even if you don't remember who that is right now. Sometimes it's what we perceive to be the most destructive that is actually clearing the way for us to truly see. For all the answers we seek are inside of us. We are a constant evolution.

And although we can see and begin to remove the identity cloaks, it isn't easy. The cloaks may come on and off for many years, until one day, the ones that don't fit are placed on the hook, we hesitantly walk away, and vow never again to put them back on. No permission needed. A knowing in your heart that it is not for you. But some cloaks are comfortable. There when we need them; but never smothering. Able to come on and off freely – less identity, and more who we choose to be in the world. And we can't make that wrong. They have protected us. Reminded us of our beautifully vulnerable humanness.

I am the good girl. The reliable one. The responsible one. The one who keeps her shit together. Identities I have clung to so tightly. Less now for others. For my own comfort. The truth is, no-one is asking me to be anyone other than my true self. In all my flaws. My identity is telling me to put a nice, neat bow on my words, to pull them all together and say the lesson is that freedom comes when we choose our soul over our identity. But that's not life. We are human and it is a constant dance. I am not free from my identity. It's often comfortable, and then exhausting. And I give myself permission to uncloak, to lay it all down when it gets too heavy. Trusting my soul to always lead me home.

I am often hidden; but never lost.

I am becoming; and unbecoming.

I am here.

I am alive.

NATALIE SIMES lives by the premise 'you are not loved for what you do, but for who you are'. Now in her 40s, she has been on a journey back to herself, determined to live a life of no regrets. A few wake-up calls with the presence of Motor Neurone Disease and Huntington's Disease in her family, Natalie made the decision that she doesn't want to play safe anymore. Natalie loves to spend time with her husband and children, as well as reading, exploring new places, and travelling all over to support her children's sporting endeavours! As a writer, personal mentor and retreat facilitator, Natalie hopes to create deep connections through her writing, giving others the permission and support to return to, and be seen for, who they truly are.

@nataliesimeswrites

THE PILGRIMAGE TO THE HOME WITHIN

ASHLEE CANDY SAM

To Cambodians everywhere
and fellow cycle breakers.

Where is home? They say home is where the heart is and that is within.

But how do we get there? We must start the courageous journey of the pilgrimage to the home within. We start by searching for the stories that are felt within our bloodlines, told by our ancestors. We gently float into the gentle tides of our sacred waters. We listen to the whispers of the soul. As we journey along, we find ourselves interconnected in soul, mind, body and history.

As I sit in the comfort of my mother's home, I am sitting across from our family altar. There are framed faces that seem to have not aged a day, as they've been photographed during a moment where time stood still. The current faces on the family altar are my father, my grandfather from my father's side and both of my grandparents on my mother's side. Alongside these photos are candles, small indoor plants, a rice-filled glass cup with burnt-out incense sticks, and a Buddha statue – all on top of an altar cloth. This altar that honours my passed loved ones reminds me of my lineage and the legacy I want to leave behind as a future ancestor.

Understanding myself meant understanding all the layers within me. Without going too deep into the stories of who I am, as this is worthy of more than just a chapter, finding my home within meant understanding the internal battles I faced. The challenges, obstacles, drama, trauma – whatever you want to call it. I was drowning in it from a young age and for a while, all I could feel was darkness; held down in the void of overwhelm and helplessness. But I somehow found glimmering gems of wisdom beneath them all. One of the layers I will explore here is the layer of my lineage.

Being a first-generation Cambodian born in Australia, my upbringing felt complex. My parents were raising us in a completely different world to theirs, in a land that wasn't their first home.

Although I was born in Sydney, Australia, both my parents were born in a province called Battambang in Cambodia. Their decision to come to Australia was no choice of their own. Both were born in the year 1970 and only stayed until 1975–1976. Why? Because of the Pol Pot regime. Pol Pot was the leader of the Khmer Rouge and ruled Cambodia between 1975 and 1979. This communist regime was a ruthless and unforgivable act of violence that saw more than a million people killed by the hands of the Khmer Rouge. Yes, the Khmer Rouge were Cambodians who followed Pol Pot's lead. To survive, they were coerced, or joined for ideological reasons, while others were very young conscripts. I encourage you to do your own research into our history to fully understand what my people have endured; to also witness the rise that comes from acts of survival, strength and resilience.

My parents arrived in Australia around six years of age and met each other during their high school years. Their love story is something you'd see from a teenage pop show. My mother was fashionable, smart, obedient and kind, and my father was also fashionable, rebellious and caring. I was told by his best friend that he used to skip school to visit my mother during school hours. Their love grew through having a mutual connection from being Cambodian – coincidentally, both were born in the same province – their love for music and food. Their love continued to grow even fonder, and as a result, I was born in May 1994.

Growing up and living in Australia has been bliss. Despite the challenges of mundane responsibilities that seem to be never-ending as an adult, the mundane is a privilege. My father had always told my younger brother and me to take advantage of opportunities that fell before us. I was privileged enough to learn and play the violin at five years old, and also participated in taekwondo lessons. I remember so many fun memories from childhood. The camping trips, weekend barbeques, sleeping over at my grandparents' house. All of these memories are so warm and full of love. There were also temple visits during Cambodian New Year, Ancestor Day (Pchum Ben) and any funerals we attended. Visiting the temples was always exciting, whatever the circumstances. As a child, it was hard to sit through the monks chanting prayer, but the adults would always let us know when we could run off to play around the temple. We knew Cambodian New Year meant big celebrations and night stalls full of Cambodian street-style food and drinks, desserts, trinkets and toys.

While I enjoyed a lot of my upbringing, there are always more sides to every story. When I was around the age of ten years old, home started to feel less as a home. There were echoes of anger, shouting and arguments, shattering plates, vibrations of slamming doors. I felt isolated and misunderstood, so I started shutting down. I began to wear a mask to hide these battles that I was facing. I also experienced bullying, and it made my world darker than it already was. I was fifteen years old, trying to navigate these difficult situations, and I was losing hope that it would ever get better.

At my father's funeral day, I was told I wasn't allowed to participate in some of the ceremonial rituals due to cultural beliefs. I was only allowed to offer prayer with the monks at the beginning of the ceremony. I remember thinking, *why does the world continue to be cruel to me?* I deserve closure. I just couldn't receive it the same way as everyone else. After his funeral, my visits to the temples became limited as I was struggling to find the courage or meaning to be there anymore.

At this point of my life, my vision of the world became clouded with doubt and sadness. However, this grief catapulted my journey for self-discovery and reconnecting to my culture. There was so much of myself that I left behind in the darkness. Before this journey back to self through reclamation of my lineage, I felt undeserving, small, that I wasn't allowed to take up space. I continued to grow through an array of life lessons thrown at me. My nearest and dearest have always said to me, 'Ashlee, you are the strongest person I know. You can literally make it through anything and everything because you always do.'

I spent months with psychiatrists and psychologists in my late twenties to safely unravel the layers of my traumas and walls of protection. I found myself leaning into my intuition and connecting to my spirit. I delved into the world of channelling messages through divine guidance with oracle/tarot cards. I learnt about breathwork, affirmations and meditations. And through Reiki healing meditations with careful loving hands of practitioners who I now call my friends, I found my circle of healed, wise and well ancestors.

Ancestors. This kept calling me.

In the same upstairs living room in my mother's home, I stumbled across an Instagram live from an account that focuses on ancestral healing. As I watched the livestream, my spirit lit up inside and I knew that this was the type of healing my soul had been yearning for. Without hesitation, I signed up to a six-week online course to learn about what it means to heal ancestral wounds and lines. During the six weeks, it was a journey that was profound and honestly healed me in so many ways. I learnt about epigenetics and how intergenerational trauma is also passed on through DNA; that we are so much more than our current family's ancestry. Our ancestry dates back thousands and thousands of years, and honestly, I think it's so wonderful. It's wonderful to know that we are generations made from the continuation of love and hope. I felt like I finally understood everything.

In this course, I remember two things I won't ever forget. They are 'look through life with eyes of love and compassion' and 'with every challenge, there is always a gem of wisdom.' These have imprinted on my soul and it allows me to stay aligned with my way of living.

Let's fast forward to now.

I recently travelled to Cambodia. My last visit before then was sixteen years ago. During this trip, I felt such a strong calling to come back home. To come back and reconnect with animism, Theravada Buddhism and with the land that holds atrocities; to learn from the resilience, courage and strength that my people showed in the face of fear and displacement. I was there for just over a week, so we had a jam-packed itinerary. In Cambodia, I was joined by my partner, cousin and her husband. I couldn't have had it any other way. They were open to explore, learn and witness what Cambodia is outside of its grim history.

This visit in particular will always hold a special place in my heart. Returning as a woman, now in my thirties, and truly understanding what it means to be of Cambodian descent, faced with all the battles I endured, it reminded me of my true essence and I wouldn't be here without those who came before me. Although Battambang is my parents' hometown and I'm yet to visit there again, being in Siem Reap felt like home. I recall sending my mother a message saying I have finally made it to Cambodia.

She asked me, 'How does it feel being there?'

I replied, 'I almost cried on landing and it just feels like home.'

Despite the lack of Cambodian that I can speak, the locals' eyes shone brighter than stars, with smiles wider than you can measure, when they found out that I was a Cambodian child coming home to visit. Some even thanked me for trying to speak the language and for remembering our culture.

We spent most of our time in Siem Reap visiting temples all around. This truly fed my soul. It made me feel whole again. The lands, the earth, the history, the architecture, the teachings. This part of the trip felt like it recharged me for what was to come next, which was our trip to Phnom Penh where I had booked a day tour to visit the Killing Fields and S-21 Museum. This is where so much of my own strength, vulnerability and heart remained open.

The day that we visited the Killing Fields and S-21 Museum, all I did was cry. I cried in pure grief and anger because now I could truly understand what my family endured to come to Australia to survive. I messaged my mother again, this time with words of grief and gratitude. She remembers the dark times, and most of the Khmer Rouge survivors don't want to remember these times. It's easier to forget about it when you live through it, and that's OK. There are some survivors who are strong enough to come out and share their stories and help heal through storytelling.

If someone were to ask you, 'What kind of ancestor do you want to be?' would you know how to answer?

My answer: I want to be an ancestor who is full of love, kindness and compassion. The one who breaks cycles of harm, discontent and unmeaningful projections. The one who remembers that strength can be found within oneself and shared across communities. Who leads with action of high intentions, only for the highest of good.

I want to be the type of ancestor who continues to honour her lineage, celebrating culture, ritual and ceremonies. Because I cannot risk losing it and only finding it in forgotten history books. I want to be the ancestor where children will remember me for the softness, nurturance, gentleness they needed. I want to be the ancestor who always brings calmness and a quiet, safe home, no matter where they are. I want to be an ancestor who will encourage and inspire others to live with similar beliefs. That despite any harmful actions from someone, they are still deserving of love and compassion because we all deserve to heal. In a world that's still out of balance, be an ancestor who will continue to promote all things good.

I returned home, back to Australia, with a fuller and wiser heart. A heart that made it back home to herself with true connection with her motherland. I am reminded that my journey has chosen me because my spirit knows that I am strong enough to continue breaking cycles. I'm feeling a stronger sense of purpose to my being here in this lifetime, and I am grateful for the opportunity this has brought to allow me to start this larger and wider journey of storytelling.

ASHLEE CANDY SAM is a certified Reiki Master - 3A, which allows her to provide services and offerings such as Intuitive-Reiki infused healing meditations, oracle and tarot card readings and group journaling circles. Her journeys throughout this lifetime have given her strength, wisdom, deep understanding and compassion. She is deeply connected and rooted in remembering ancestral practices that help her stay aligned with her values and goals. Part of her goals in life is to continue to share and hold safe space for individuals, to allow them to feel safe in vulnerability and encourage them to journey within to either start or continue their healing journey and to continue learning about epigenetics and the effects this has on intergenerational trauma carried through DNA.

HER

FERRIS

Dedicated to me. For me.
To my husband and children, you will continue to inspire me every day.
I love you.

I thought about the million things I could write, especially around one story. But I want that story to end. I am turning forty-two in a week. The Leo baby. The eldest daughter. The wife. The mother. The storyteller. As I showered this morning, tears fell. I felt her. Breaking through. She is coming back. Deep in my soul, a remembering and understanding of who it is to be her.

I have spent the morning deep in conversation with not only myself but a friend. *What happened to me, to her?* As I reflected on my journey through womanhood, I realised that I'm finally at a stage in my life where it's silent. This is my stage of deep gratitude. For myself.

This is a time of untangling the grief that swells within me like a dark passenger. I have carried the weight of a million worlds on my shoulders. Seen and unseen. Known and unknown. My husband is working, my children are in school, and the house is quiet. A silence I have missed. Finally, I can hear myself. The leaves blow in the wind as the neighbours move in, and I can hear my bulldog snore. Fresh flowers on my messy table, as always, covered with crystals and incense. This week's card, which is The Hierophant, sits front row and centre on a tiny art easel. Fitting for the moments.

Silence. This gives me time to think, to reflect, to breathe it all in. To feel the pain I am left with after everything. *You didn't need to be strong.* You needed to feel it all like you did, and that is OK. *You made it, you are here.* Everything that has been my life. From childhood to teenage loss, to family destruction and self-sabotage. To becoming a mother, to looking death in the eyes for years. To having no control. To stepping back into the quiet, to asking myself who am I now? Feeling sadness and isolation like never before. A loss on levels only I can understand. Asking her to come back, inviting her to step so beautifully forward. Fully. I see her in the shadows. Her brown eyes look back at me, the loose curls fall from her bun, and the millions of freckles on her face all smoosh into one. I see her, carefree, deep love in her heart, nestled in a tree, staring at the stars.

As I roll into my early-forties, I reflect on the friendships I've lost, the beautiful ones that made me feel like home no matter what, and the people who landed like a missing piece. I reflect on the time I've lost. I reflect on the lessons learned. There are regrets around what choices I made, and there are things I wish I could change. But at the end of the day, they are my story.

My life. Her life. A part of me. Giving myself grace for what I didn't know. Releasing more of the deep guilt I hold onto deep within my heart. Locked up like a prisoner. It is time to let go. Let go of it all.

Today I am a week from my forty-second birthday. Forty-two years in this crazy place. What an honour it is to have experienced these days. I sit here in my kitchen, and over and over, I have written my chapter. But each time, I realised that was not it. I realised it was just me pulling apart another layer of who and what I really want to share, what words need to come to the paper. What is my story waiting to be shared? I realised I needed to leave it to the last minute to fully evolve into where I wanted it to go. I could sit here and repeat the story. The story that has been burnt into my soul like a branded bull in a paddock. The story you can't escape. I wanted to write it to let it go, to help myself heal these deep-rooted wounds. But that's the thing, I don't want to repeat the story. I am tired of my story. I want that cycle to end, and as my spiritual glow flutters in the back of my mind and I realise deeply who I am, the more that story disappears into the moonlight. Each time I wrote, it was like a Band-Aid ripping another layer off. I was untangling all that I was, that I am, and that I am becoming.

As I feel a presence like I never have before, I realise this is my chapter.

I am not *just* a mother. I am *all* the mothers who walked before me. I am my mother, and my mother's mother. All the grandmothers live inside me, and as every part of me breaks apart, more of me comes back home to my soul. I see them in me. I feel them around me as I prepare meals, and smile as I smell them pass by. Their strength inside me is also their stories. Their voices quiet for so long, vibrating through, asking me to speak. My soul craves the deep words to come to paper and express all of her being. All of our being. Here and now. I'm reflecting on how the challenges have shaped me. The endless challenges that come in waves and like the ocean, swallowed me whole. Drowning me. I lost myself in the chaos of parenthood, trauma and the expectations of who I am supposed to be. Managing a business, holding a job, and being a parent all the while, living in the hospital wards. Life is complex, and unpredictable. It is full of seen and unseen pressures. Who society tells you to be, and in a way who your parents shape you to be. It consumes you. *Am I making them proud? Am I doing the right thing? What does everyone think of me? I can't do that! You can't do that!* My daughter has a disease now known as VIPER. Named after her. That is a big part of my story, but it isn't my story to tell.

The memories will forever tell my tale, but those stories I tell myself change now inside me as I carve the way for my daughters and son to see a better way of living. That love comes from actions, more than words. I don't need to have it together, and will never ever be ready. I will forever be leaning in and learning about myself, unravelling another part as my subconscious mind delivers more signs. I will not stop the crumble. When the wheels turn, pulling me forward in ways I never experienced, I feel it. The remembering of my soul. The inner child, the goddess screaming for attention. The stories and feeling of freedom that need to be remembered so I can truly feel her essence. She. Her. Woman. Mother. Keeper.

What an honour to be here on beautiful Mother Earth – her sunlight upon my skin, the sound of the ocean waves, the birds, the sounds that calm my nervous system like a baby in a mother's hold. It has been ten years of medical-mum life. But now I am here, living by the seaside in a small country town that I have had in my dreams for years. The visions of the whales carrying me and my family from the depths of the ocean floor to a calm beach, where we lie on the sand. A small town in the distance. Home. From drowning to beginning again. My spirit speaks louder than ever. The lungs are clear, and the healing has truly begun. As words weave magic spells, and rituals become life. A magic swims within. Her magic breathes new life. She is finally here. Stepping into her being, stepping back into her body as the woman she once knew she would be. I acknowledge all that it is. Every cell. I listen to her song as she weaves magic into my veins. The guilt that rips apart her heart, the fear that sneaks around her mind like a ghost. This is her. She is ugly. She is angry. She is her. The ticking of clocks on a white wall is a distant memory, the beeping of oxygen machines, and the scurry of nurses in and out as your eyes burn from sleep deprivation. You're huddled on a hospital floor, maybe a chair, and the ache from the forty-eight hours of being awake echoes through every cell of your body. This is no longer our story, just a part of our story. A chapter in a book that will always lead back to something magical. That will always open portals into other dimensions.

I give her grace for the endless nights she held her babies alone in hospital wards, on bedroom floors and the days her bones wouldn't even let her move. The times she cried when no one could see, and the days she felt completely lost and unseen. When the days all blurred into one, and the guilt destroyed her. Now, she doesn't recognise her reflection, and anxiety blurs her vision as she dreams of a better life. I see you in all your raw, untamed magic. The messy, drunken teen in another field, with your sweetheart. The blackout drunk in her twenties, disconnecting from her teen-self. I married my high school sweetheart. Forever friends. I still feel the wind in my hair as he would dink me across the bridge on his bike after school, and the secret sessions we had on the bench seat of his WB. Tucked away on the riverside in the bushland. Engulfed in each other's arms. Skin on skin. The windows fogged, and the giggles loud, as the stars reflected in the river. Freedom in all her glory, with nights spent gazing at stars, and the campfire burning.

But she can no longer do this. Forever carrying everyone. The people pleaser.

Putting aside her own hopes, dreams, desires, words for fear of upsetting someone.

But then she did … I reflect on the days when I planned to finish our marriage. That it was time to take my power back for myself. It was time to change the story. Break the cycle.

We are rewriting our story. We have lived thousands of lives together, and this one we are getting right. We challenged the systems, and we ran the gauntlet together.

She travelled Australia, and felt the timelines shift in the gorges. She floated with turtles in the crystal waters, she danced with a brolga, she floated in gorges as kookaburras sang. She found herself over and over again. She is the wildling taking charge again, the soul dancing with spirit, the mother sharing her stories, and slowing it all down to be seen. She is the volcano erupting and the flowers in your hair. Celebrate her. She has carried you every inch.

I call her back, in all her fearlessness, her feralness, and all her power. I call her back.

The mother. The keeper. She is me. I am her. Welcome home.

FERRIS, known to her parents as Sarah, Sezzy, or Mag, is a 42 year old mother of three who grew up in regional Victoria, where her deep connection to nature, family, spirit and freedom first took root. She's not a published writer by trade, but a lifelong lover of words (including all the swearing), the kind that stir the soul and leave a trace on the heart. You can find her drowning in crystals, and cacao or walking beach side in her home on the Queensland coast. With a creative mind and a fierce spirit, Ferris finds magic in the everyday and beauty in what others overlook. Her work is shaped by intuition, healing, family and the messy, magnificent journey of being human. Let her word's drop into your soul, and weave a spell.

@theshed888

We are made up of stories. They wait in silence to be told.
May *Anthologia* inspire you to tell yours.

www.thekindpress.com